Equality in Law between Men and Women in the European Community

Portugal

Equality in Law between Men and Women in the European Community

Series Editors

MICHEL VERWILGHEN
Professeur ordinaire à la Faculté de Droit
Université catholique de Louvain

FERDINAND VON PRONDZYNSKI
Professor of Law and Dean of the Law School
The University of Hull

European Commission

Equality in Law between Men and Women in the European Community

Portugal

by

Teresa MARTINS de OLIVEIRA
Licenciée en Droit
Avocat au Barreau de Bruxelles

MARTINUS NIJHOFF PUBLISHERS
DORDRECHT/BOSTON/LONDON

OFFICE FOR OFFICIAL PUBLICATIONS OF THE EUROPEAN COMMUNITIES
LUXEMBOURG

A C.I.P. Catalogue record for this book is available from the Library of Congress.

ISBN (this volume) 0-7923-1838-2 (Martinus Nijhoff Publishers)
92-826-4476-6 (Office for Official Publications of the EC)

This study was commissioned by the Equal Opportunities Unit of Directorate-General V (Employment, Industrial Relations and Social Affairs) of the European Commission. It does not, however, express the Commission's official views. The responsibility for the views expressed lies with the authors.

A French version of this text has been published by the Office for Official Publications of the European Communities and Les Editions Juridiques Bruylant, Brussels.

Published by

Office for Official Publications of the European Communities, L-2985 Luxembourg

ISBN (this volume) 92-826-4476-6 Catalogue number CE-97-92-011-EN-C

and

Martinus Nijhoff Publishers,

P.O. Box 163, 3300 AD Dordrecht, The Netherlands

ISBN (series) 0-7923-1842-0 ISBN (this volume) 0-7923-1838-2

Sold and distributed for the Office for Official Publications of the European Communities by the distributors listed on the inside back cover.

Kluwer Academic Publishers incorporates the publishing programmes of D. Reidel, Martinus Nijhoff, Dr W. Junk and MTP Press.

Sold and distributed in the USA and Canada
by Kluwer Academic Publishers,
101 Philip Drive, Norwell, MA 02061, U.S.A.

In all other countries sold and distributed
by Kluwer Academic Publishers Group,
P.O. Box 322, 3300 AH Dordrecht, The Netherlands

Printed in Belgium

TABLE OF CONTENTS

		Page
Foreword		xi
Notice to the reader		xv
Abbreviations		xvii
Table of legislation etc.		xix
Table of cases		xxv

COMMENTARY ON EQUALITY LAW

1. GENERAL ... 3

1.1 Introduction ... 3
- 1.1.1 Introduction to the national legal system ... 3
- 1.1.2 Economic and social context ... 4

1.2 Sources ... 6
- 1.2.1 International standards ... 6
  - 1.2.1.1 Human rights ... 6
  - 1.2.1.2 Treaties on special questions ... 6
- 1.2.2 European Community law ... 7
  - 1.2.2.1 Direct effect of Community law ... 7
  - 1.2.2.2 Retrospective implementation ... 8
- 1.2.3 Constitutional law ... 9
- 1.2.4 Legislation ... 10
  - 1.2.4.1 Prior legislation ... 10
  - 1.2.4.2 Present legislation ... 11

2. BASIC CONCEPTS ... 13

2.1 The concepts of equality and discrimination ... 13

2.2 Direct discrimination ... 14
- 2.2.1 Definition ... 14
  - 2.2.1.1 Reason ... 14
  - 2.2.1.2 Detriment ... 14
  - 2.2.1.3 Comparator ... 15
- 2.2.2 Extended definition ... 15
  - 2.2.2.1 Marital status ... 15
  - 2.2.2.2 Family status ... 15
  - 2.2.2.3 Pregnancy ... 15
  - 2.2.2.4 Sexual harassment ... 15
  - 2.2.2.5 Physical attributes ... 16
  - 2.2.2.6 Dress codes ... 16

2.3 Indirect discrimination ... 16
- 2.3.1 Definition ... 16
- 2.3.2 Suspect criteria ... 17
- 2.3.3 Disproportionate impact ... 17
- 2.3.4 Objective justification ... 18

2.4 Victimization ... 18

3. EQUAL PAY 19

3.1 Principle 19

3.2 Exceptions 19
3.2.1 Size 19
3.2.2 Work done outside the jurisdiction 19
3.2.3 Health and safety 20
3.2.4 National security 20
3.2.5 Religion, religious schools 20
3.2.6 Retirement age 20

3.3 Personal scope of principle 20
3.3.1 Employees 20
3.3.2 Independent contractors 20
3.3.3 Home workers 21
3.3.4 Public sector 21
3.3.5 Domestic employees 21
3.3.6 Non-employed population 21

3.4 Activities covered 21

3.5 Definition of remuneration 21
3.5.1 Article 119 of the EEC Treaty 21
3.5.2 Fringe benefits 22
3.5.3 Contributions by employer 22
3.5.4 Contributions by employee 22
3.5.5 Post-contribution benefits 22
3.5.6 Pensions 22
3.5.7 Collective agreements 22

3.6 Comparator 23
3.6.1 Same establishment 23
3.6.2 Contemporaneous employment 23
3.6.3 Hypothetical male 23
3.6.4 Different establishment/same employer 23
3.6.5 Cross-industry comparisons 23

3.7 Woman does same work as man 23
3.7.1 Identical work 23
3.7.2 Similar work 23
3.7.3 Night-work 24

3.8 Equal value 24
3.8.1 Job evaluation 24
3.8.2 Job classification 24
3.8.2.1 Factors 24
3.8.2.2 Weightings 24
3.8.2.3 Traditional male/female 24
3.8.3 Higher value 25
3.8.4 Proportionate pay 25

3.9 Legitimate reason for pay differential 25
3.9.1 Material difference 25
3.9.2 Economic benefits/market forces 25
3.9.3 Night-work 25
3.9.4 Part-time work 25
3.9.5 Red circles 26

3.10 Levelling up/down 26

4. EQUAL TREATMENT 27

4.1 Principle 27

4.2 Exceptions 27
4.2.1. Exclusions 27
4.2.1.1 Size 27
4.2.1.2 Work done outside the jurisdiction 27
4.2.1.3 Health and safety 27
4.2.1.4 National security 27
4.2.1.5 Religion, religious schools 28
4.2.1.6 Retirement age 28
4.2.2. Sex as a determining factor 28
4.2.2.1 Lists 28
4.2.2.2 Genuine occupational qualification 29
4.2.2.3 Authenticity 29
4.2.2.4 Security 29
4.2.2.5 Religion 29
4.2.2.6 Decency and privacy 29
4.2.2.7 Single-sex establishments 30

4.3 Territorial scope 30

4.4 Personal scope 30
4.4.1 Employees 30
4.4.2 Independent contractors 30
4.4.3 Home workers 30
4.4.4 Public sector 30
4.4.5 Domestic employees 30
4.4.6 Non-employed population 30
4.4.7 Other workers 31

4.5 Activities covered 31

4.6 Comparator 31

4.7 Hiring 31
4.7.1 Recruitment methods 31
4.7.2 Advertisements 31
4.7.3 Job title 32
4.7.4 Job description 32
4.7.5 Selection arrangements 32
4.7.6 Terms on which a job is offered 32
4.7.7 Refusal or deliberate omission to offer a job 32

4.8 Working conditions 32
4.8.1 Relation to pay 32
4.8.2 Education and training 33
4.8.3 Access to benefits, facilities, services, promotion 34

4.9 Exclusion, dismissal or other detriment 34
4.9.1 Disciplinary sanctions 34
4.9.2 Dismissal 34

4.10 Instructions to discriminate 35

4.11 Pressure to discriminate 35

4.12 Discrimination by an employee or a trade union 35

4.13 Discriminatory practices 35

4.14 Special treatment 36
4.14.1 Protective legislation 36

4.14.1.1 Pregnancy and maternity 36
4.14.1.2 Parental leave and analogous measures 36
4.14.1.3 Difficult or unpleasant working conditions 37
4.14.2 Positive action 37
4.14.2.1 Definition 37
4.14.2.2 Field of application 37
4.14.2.3 Means 38
4.14.2.4 Constitutional or legal problems 38

5. SOCIAL SECURITY 41

5.1 Definition of social security 41
5.1.1 Statutory social security 41
5.1.2 Occupational social security 41
5.1.3 Social assistance 42

5.2 Social security directives and other legislation 42
5.2.1 Article 119 of the EEC Treaty 42
5.2.2 Directive 75/117/EEC 42
5.2.3 Directive 76/207/EEC 43
5.2.4 Directive 79/7/EEC 43
5.2.5 Directive 86/613/EEC 43

5.3 Problematic concepts 43
5.3.1 Breadwinner 43
5.3.2 Sole breadwinner 43
5.3.3 Head of household 43
5.3.4 Cohabitant 44
5.3.5 Living alone 44
5.3.6 Dependant 44

5.4 Exceptions 44
5.4.1 Retirement age 44
5.4.2 Sex as a determining factor 44

5.5 Levelling up/down 45

5.6 Part-time work 45

6. ENFORCEMENT OF THE PRINCIPLE 47

6.1 Court or tribunal procedure 47
6.1.1 Acquiring the evidence 47
6.1.1.1 Prescribed forms 47
6.1.1.2 Obligation to furnish all relevant evidence 47
6.1.1.3 Annual information to works councils 47
6.1.2. Burden of proof 47
6.1.3 Costs 48
6.1.4 Legal aid 48
6.1.5 Remedies 48
6.1.5.1 Nullity/annulment 48
6.1.5.2 Termination of discriminatory conduct 49
6.1.5.3 Declaration 49
6.1.5.4 Compensation 49
6.1.5.5 Recommendation 49
6.1.5.6 Positive enforceable order 49
6.1.5.7 Positive action plan 49
6.1.5.8 Criminal and administrative sanctions 49
6.1.6 Class actions 50
6.1.7 Exclusion of judicial redress 50
6.1.8 Time limits 50

6.2 Courts and tribunals ... 50
6.2.1 Specialized jurisdiction ... 50
6.2.1.1 Equality officer ... 51
6.2.1.2 Arbitration court ... 51
6.2.1.3 Equal opportunities agency ... 51
6.2.1.4 Conciliation procedures ... 51
6.2.2 Specialized training for judges ... 51
6.2.3 Specialization within the system ... 51

6.3 Enforcement agency ... 52
6.3.1 Type ... 52
6.3.1.1 Labour inspectorate ... 52
6.3.1.2 Equal opportunities agency ... 52
6.3.2 Functions ... 52
6.3.2.1 Advice ... 52
6.3.2.2 Research ... 53
6.3.2.3 Legal aid ... 53
6.3.3 Remedies ... 53
6.3.3.1 Notice ... 53
6.3.3.2 Injunction ... 53
6.3.3.3 Compensation ... 54

6.4 Collective agreements ... 54
6.4.1 Equal pay clause ... 54
6.4.2 Automatic nullity ... 54
6.4.3 Collective redress ... 54
6.4.4 Agency monitoring ... 55

SOURCES OF EQUALITY LAW

7. LEGISLATION ... 59

7.1 Constitutional provisions ... 59
7.1.1 Constitution of 2 April 1976 ... 59

7.2 National laws ratifying international treaties ... 61

7.3 National texts implementing EC Directives ... 62
7.3.1 Provisions relevant to equal pay and equal treatment ... 63
7.3.1.1 Decree (DL) No 392/79 ... 63
7.3.2 Provisions relevant to equal pay ... 66
7.3.2.1 Decree (DL) No 392/79 ... 66
7.3.3 Provisions relevant to equal treatment ... 67
7.3.3.1 Decree (DL) No 392/79 ... 67
7.3.3.2 Law No 4/84 ... 69
7.3.3.3 Decree (DL) No 135/85 ... 73
7.3.3.4 Decree (DL) No 136/85 ... 73
7.3.3.5 Decree (DL) No 154/88 ... 73
7.3.4 Provisions relevant to equality in social security ... 74
7.3.4.1 Law No 28/84 ... 74

7.4 Other national texts ... 76
7.4.1 Decree (DL) No 409/71 ... 76
7.4.2 Decrees (DL) No 251/74, No 308/74, No 492/74 ... 77
7.4.3 Decree (DL) No 166/91 ... 77
7.4.4 Decree (DL) No 451/91 ... 78
7.4.5 Decree (DL) No 496/77 ... 79
7.4.6 Decree (DL) No 330/90 ... 79

8. CASES ... 81

8.1 Decisions on the principle of equality ... 81

8.2 Decisions on equal pay ... 81

8.3 Decisions on equal treatment ... 89

8.4 Decisions on equality in social security ... 93

9. DOCUMENTATION ... 99

9.1 Bibliography ... 99
9.1.1 Books ... 99
9.1.2 Articles, notes and reports ... 99

9.2 Information ... 104
9.2.1 Activities of the Comissão da Condição Feminina ... 104
9.2.2 Activities of the Comissão da Condição Feminina and its consultative committee ... 105
9.2.3 Useful addresses ... 106

INDEX ... 107

FOREWORD

Since the Second World War several international organizations have been endeavouring to promote the principle of equal opportunities between women and men, in law as well as in practice. This objective has also been pursued in a number of countries within the framework of domestic law. The intention has been to pursue a social objective and to achieve a change in the patterns of social conduct. In this context it has been felt that where the law visibly adopts the principle of equality this may contribute to the transformation of attitudes.

It has generally been accepted that equal opportunities ought to be pursued in the working environment in particular. In part this is because employment equality is a concept which can be more easily addressed by legal means than can other aspects of equality, but it is also true that a better distribution of wealth and income between the sexes and the abandonment of separate gender roles in the labour market can provide a powerful impetus to the realization of equal opportunities in society more generally.

To some extent these initiatives have been successful. Progress has been made in a relatively short space of time, although perhaps in limited areas of the equal opportunities agenda. But the impact has been restricted, and much effort still needs to be made in order to improve both law and social practice.

* * *

Within the European Community also there has been a steady growth of interest in the issue of equality between women and men. Article 119 of the Treaty instituting the European Economic Community, signed in Rome on 25 March 1957, provides for equal pay for women and men workers who perform equal work. The main Directive advancing the idea of equal pay, Directive 75/117/EEC, will soon be celebrating its twentieth birthday.

But it is not enough to enact Directives. It is also necessary to analyse and control the implementation of these texts in the Member States of the European Community. The Commission of the European Communities has obviously understood this, since in its Action Programme for 1982-1985 it placed particular emphasis on the need to follow up the implementation of the Equality Directives. In pursuit of this the Commission established a number of expert networks to consider the equality agenda from a variety of viewpoints. One of these networks was the Network of Experts on the Implementation of the Equality Directives, consisting of experts from each of the Member States of the Community.

These experts have drawn up a series of reports on various aspects of their remit, and have been able to offer advice to the Commission on desirable courses of action to be followed. The network has also met regularly to discuss the reports and to update the Commission and each other on important developments in each of the Member States. Some of the network's consolidated reports have been published by the European Commission, and indeed the information contained in network documentation has been used in conferences of legal practitioners and other interested persons organized under the auspices of the Commission. However, the national reports written by network members remain unpublished and are unavailable to the general public.

In fact these reports form an excellent source of legislative and jurisprudential information from the Member States in matters of equality. They shed light on the progress made and the work which remains to be done if we are to achieve equality both in law and in practice. The experts therefore expressed the desire to see their work published and widely disseminated in the European Community and internationally, so that it can be used to assist not only legal practitioners but also other groups and persons seeking to achieve the objective of equal opportunities.

However, the reports drawn up for the network could not necessarily have been published in the form in which they were produced. Their authors had drawn up working documents, rather than studies designed for publication. Furthermore network members were, at any rate initially, given significant discretion as to how the work should be produced. From 1986 onwards a common format based on agreed schemas was devised to give network reports greater homogeneity, and this also prompted a growing desire to produce a more extensive collection of knowledge in this field.

The European Commission therefore decided to promote the progressive publication of an encyclopædia on equality in law between women and men in the European Community. This was to consist of volumes which were no longer to be only administrative documents intended for Commission use, but were to present a high level of scientific and formal quality.

There is no need to discuss at length the importance and interest of such a publication, which forms a natural part of the Commission's programme of action regarding the promotion of equality of opportunity. In fact it represents an excellent method of consolidating Community knowledge of existing legal provisions in order to ensure their better implementation. It represents also the desire to extend and develop the traditional means of disseminating information, in such a way as to sensitize the public more effectively.

The plans for such an encyclopædia were formulated by experts attending the Spanish Presidency seminar on equal opportunities in Toledo in April 1989.

It was with much pleasure that the coordinators of this major project have been able to witness the gradual production of the volumes in this collection. Nevertheless, in spite of all the care take by the experts involved in this work, the encyclopædia is neither exhaustive, perfect nor definitive, since the law continues to evolve. However, it is hoped that it will prove useful to all those — judges, tribunal members, lawyers, civil servants, teachers and researchers — who are interested in this subject.

* * *

The present volume, pertaining to Portuguese law, is an integral part of the encyclopædia. It was therefore prepared on the basis of a structure common to all volumes in the series, in order to allow for a comparative reading of the law in each Member State on equality between women and men. The volume states the law as at 1 November 1992.

The first part of the volume — the Commentary — is based on a detailed plan common to all the national volumes, drawn up in such a way as to allow the reader to adopt a comparative approach. This plan draws both on the characteristics of the legal systems in use in the States linked to the Roman-Germanic legal tradition and in those following the common law tradition. One result of this is that certain headings may not be relevant to the position in each Member State.

The rest of the volume contains legislative texts actually in force in Portugal which implement the principles laid down in the EC Equality Directives, as well as the most significant court and tribunal decisions applying those texts.

* * *

The coordinators wish to express their gratitude to all those who have lent their assistance and support to the encyclopædia project, and to show particular appreciation to certain of them.

We need to record our gratitude to the authors, without whom this work would not have been produced. The essential quality of the encyclopædia lies in the work of its main authors; they spared no effort in the assembling of the necessary documentation and in drawing up an intelligible and useful commentary.

A particular word of thanks is due to the staff of the Equal Opportunities Unit of DG V of the European Commission. Since the project was discussed in the initial stages a large number of officials have been associated with it and have provided active assistance and support to the coordinators. It has been a pleasure to collaborate with the Unit.

Similarly, the coordinators would like to express their sincere thanks to the officials of the Office for Official Publications of the European Communities, whose patient and expert supervision made it possible to convert the manuscripts into publishable texts of a very high quality.

We express particular gratitude to the publishing houses which accepted the burden of the present work, which is hardly lightweight as it numbers some thirty volumes!

May this work assembled with the active participation of so many eminent and committed collaborators contribute to progress in the law, to the common good and to the promotion of formal and actual equality between the women and men of Europe.

Ferdinand von PRONDZYNSKI
Professor of Law and
Dean of the Law School
The University of Hull
United Kingdom

Michel VERWILGHEN
Professeur ordinaire
à la Faculté de Droit
Université catholique de Louvain
Belgium

NOTICE TO THE READER

The editors of the encyclopædia wish to draw the attention of the reader to certain characteristics of the collection.

1. Each volume of the encyclopædia is published in two languages, English and French. The volumes have been edited so as to ensure that they have, as far as possible, the same content and structure in their English and French versions, although the language and terminology may occasionally differ as a result of normal usage in English and French respectively.

2. The authors of the Commentary section of each volume have worked according to a common schema agreed in the European Commission's Network of Experts on the Implementation of the Equality Directives. This allows the collection as a whole to follow a uniform structure. However, the Sources section in each volume is structured according to the domestic law framework, which varies from Member State to Member State.

3. The materials contained in the Sources section of each volume have (except where the original language is English or French) been translated into the two languages of the encyclopædia. These translations are not official, though every effort has been made to provide translated versions which are of high quality and accuracy. In the event of any doubt, it will be necessary for the reader to refer to legal sources in the original language; these are the only sources of guaranteed accuracy.

4. Equality in law between women and men within the European Community is a subject affected by rapid change, in EC law as well as in the law of each Member State. The formal sources evolve so quickly that information supplied in these volumes may have to be updated from that contained in the published encyclopædia. As far as possible major legislative and jurisprudential changes which occurred during the preparation of the volumes have been indicated in footnotes. The editors hope to be able to produce regular updates at a later stage.

5. References to laws, regulations and judicial decisions follow the normal usage of the Member State from which they originate.

ABBREVIATIONS

[Expressions in square brackets are translations or explanations of the relevant Portuguese expressions or names]

1. GENERAL

art.(s)	Article(s)
CCF	*Comissão da Condição Feminina* [Commission for the Female Condition]
CGTP-IN	*Confederação Geral dos Trabalhadores Portugueses — Intersindical Nacional* [trade union federation]
CIDM	*Comissão para a Igualdade e para Direitos das Mulheres* [Commission for Equality and Women's Rights]
CITE	*Comissão para a Igualdade no Trabalho e no Emprego* [Commission for Equality at Work and in Employment]
Const.	Constitution
DL	Decreto-lei ['decree-law']
DRegul.	Decreto Regulamentar [decree]
EC	European Community/ies
ECJ	European Court of Justice
ECR	European Court Reports
EEC	European Economic Community
ESC	Escudo [Portuguese currency]
ILO	International Labour Organization/Office
P	Portaria [ministerial decree]
para.(s)	paragraph(s)
p./pp	page/pages
UGT	*União Geral de Trabalhadores* [trade union]
UN	United Nations
vol.(s)	volume(s)

2. PORTUGUESE PERIODICALS

Ac. Doutr.	*Acordãos Doutrinais do Supremo Tribunal Administrativo*
B.C.C.F.	*Boletim da Comissão da Condição Feminina*
B.M.J.	*Boletim do Ministério da Justiça*
B.T.E.	*Boletim do Trabalho e Emprego*
Col. Jurisp.	*Colectânea de Jurisprudência*
D.R.	*Diário da República* [official journal]

TABLE OF LEGISLATION ETC.

[Numbers in bold type refer to pages at which provisions are printed verbatim]

Treaties and Conventions

Council of Europe

1950 European Convention for the Protection of Human Rights and Fundamental Freedoms ... 6, 62

1961 European Social Charter ... 6-7, 62

European Communities

1957 Treaty establishing the European Economic Community

art. 119 ... 7, 21, 42

1985 Treaty of Accession (Spain and Portugal) ... 9, 62

International Labour Organization

1935 ILO Convention (No 45) on Employment of Women Underground in Mines ... 61

1948 ILO Convention (No 89) on Night Work for Women ... 61

1952 ILO Convention (No 103) on Maternity Protection ... 62

1958 ILO Discrimination (Employment and Occupation) Convention (No 111) ... 61

1971 ILO Convention (No 100) on Equal Remuneration ... 61, 82, 84

1981 ILO Convention (No 156) on Equal Opportunities for Workers with Family Responsibilities ... 62

United Nations

1948 Universal Declaration of Human Rights ... 4, 6

1966 International Covenant on Civil and Political Rights ... 6, 61

1966 International Covenant on Economic, Social and Cultural Rights ... 6, 61

1979 International Convention on the Elimination of All Forms of Discrimination against Women ... 6, 62

art. 4 ... 38

1980 Convention on the Elimination of Discrimination in Education ... 62

European Communities Secondary Legislation

1975 Directive 75/117/EEC ... 42, 62

1976 Directive 76/207/EEC ... 43, 62

1979 Directive 79/7/EEC ... 43

art. 7 ... 43

1986 Directive 86/613/EEC ... 43

Portuguese Constitution

1976 Constitution ... 3-4, 8-11, 12, 36

art. 2 ... 27

art. 8 ... 6-7, 8, 48, 91

art. 9 ... 13, 38

art. 13 ... 4, 6, 9, 13, 17, **59**, 76, 85, 91, 93-97

art. 16 ... 4, 6

art. 36 ... 9, 13

1976 Constitution (continued)
art. 47 .... 9, **59**
art. 48 .... 9, **59**
art. 52 97
art. 53 .... **59**, 84
art. 58 .... 13, 17, **59-60**, 76, 91, 97
art. 59 .... 9, 13, 19, 34, 36, 37, **60**, 84, 91
art. 60 .... 36, 91
art. 63 .... **60**
art. 67 10
art. 68 .... 10, 13, **60-61**
art. 74 .... 9, 13, 37, **61**
art. 81 9
art. 207 8
art. 276 27
art. 277 8
art. 280 8

Codes

Civil Code 11, 12
art. 1671 .... **79**
art. 1677-D **79**
Code of Labour Procedure 47, 51

Laws

Law No 2127 of 3 August 1965
Chapter XIX 93-97, 98
Law No 29/78 of 12 June 1978 .... 6, 61
Law No 45/78 of 11 July 1978 .... 6, 61
Law No 65/78 of 13 October 1978 .... 6, 62
Law No 23/80 of 26 June 1980 .... 6, 62
Law No 29/82 of 1 December 1982 27-28
art. 9 28
art. 28 28
Law No 4/84 of 5 April 1984 .... 12, 36, 73
art. 1 .... **69**
art. 2 .... **69**
art. 3 .... **69**
art. 8 .... **70**
art. 9 .... **70**
art. 10 .... **70**
art. 11 .... **71**
art. 12 .... **71**
art. 13 .... **71**
art. 14 .... 36, **71**
art. 15 .... 36, **71**
art. 16 .... **72**
art. 17 .... **72**
art. 18 .... **72**
art. 19 .... **72**
art. 20 .... 26, **73**
art. 21 .... **73**
art. 22 35

Law No 28/84 of 14 August 1984 ....41, 62
art. 2 ....**74**
art. 4 ....**74**
art. 5 ....**74**
art. 18 ....**74**
art. 19 ....**75**
art. 28 ....**75**
art. 29 ....**75**
art. 30 ....**75**
art. 33 ....**75**
art. 35 ....**76**
Law No 30/87 of 7 July 1987 ....12, 28
art. 1 28
art. 40 28
Law No 38/87 of 23 December 1987
art. 64 48

Decrees

Decree (DL) No 27891 of 26 July 1937 61
Decree (DL) No 42520 of 23 September 1959 61
Decree (DL) No 44862 of 23 January 1963 61
Decree (DRegul.) No 45266 of 23 September 1963 12
art. 88 44
Decree (DL) No 47302 of 4 November 1966 61
art. 115 82
Decree (DRegul.) No 47472 of 31 December 1966
art. 25 84
Decree (DL) No 49408 of 24 November 1969
art. 21 ....15, 18
art. 32 34
art. 33 ....34, 49
art. 40 15
art. 82 22
art. 88 22
art. 116 ....10, 82, 83
art. 118 10
art. 119 10
art. 120 10
Decree (DL) No 409/71 of 27 September 1971 ....11, 24
art. 31 ....17, **76**
art. 32 ....**76**
art. 43 25
Decree (DL) No 498/72 of 9 December 1972
art. 35 44
art. 36 44
art. 37 44
art. 38 44
Decree (DL) No 251/74 of 12 June 1974 ....12, 77
Decree (DL) No 308/74 of 6 July 1974 ....12, 77
Decree (DL) No 492/74 of 27 September 1974 ....12, 77
Decree (DL) No 112/76 of 7 February 1976 10
Decree (DL) No 485/77 of 17 November 1977 ....11, 77
Decree (DL) No 496/77 of 25 November 1977 ....12, 79
Decree (DL) No 392/79 Of 20 September 1979 ....11, 14, 19, 20, 21, 27, 30, 31, 37, 45, 62, 76, 86, 90, 92, 96, 97
art. 1 ....**63**

Decree (DL) No 392/79 (continued)
- art. 2 ... 14, 20, 21, 22, 28, 30, **63,** 87
- art. 3 ... 11, 14, 15, 17, 38, **63-64**, 76
- art. 4 ... 17, **67**, 76, 90, 96
- art. 5 ... 33, 38, **67-68**
- art. 6 ... 33, **68**
- art. 7 ... 16, 18, 19, 28, 31, 32, **68**
- art. 8 ... 11, 17, 20, 27, **68**, 76, 90
- art. 9 ... 19, 23, 24, 48, **66, 86, 87, 96**
- art. 10 ... 34, **68, 96**
- art. 11 ... 14, 18, 34, 49, **64**
- art. 12 ... 14, 26, 54, **67, 69**
- art. 13 ... 20, 54, **67**
- art. 14 ... 19, **64**
- art. 15 ... 52, 53, 55, **65**
- art. 16 ... 14, 48, 50, 54, **66**
- art. 17 ... 52
- art. 20 ... 21, 31, 62
- art. 21 ... 19
- art. 22 ... 54
- art. 23 ... 17, **66**, 76, 90

Decree (DL) No 519-C1/79 of 29 December 1979
- art. 23 ... 47
- art. 24 ... 47
- art. 43 ... 48, 55

Decree (DL) No 167/80 of 29 May 1980 ... 25
- art. 3 ... 25

Decree (DRegul.) No 112/80 of 23 October 1980 ... 62

Decree (DL) No 272-A/81 of 30 September 1981 ... 47, 51
- art. 6 ... 55
- art. 28 ... 47

Decree (DRegul.) No 12/83 of 12 February 1983 ... 42

Decree (DL) No 303/83 of 28 June 1983 ... 10
- art. 23 ... 10

Decree (DL) No 327/83 of 8 July 1983 ... 52
- art. 3 ... 52, 55
- art. 28 ... 52
- art. 29 ... 53
- art. 32 ... 53

Decree (DL) No 421/83 of 2 December 1983 ... 17
- art. 3 ... 17

Decree (DRegul.) No 63/84 of 10 October 1984 ... 62

Decree (DRegul.) No 66/84 of 11 October 1984 ... 62

Decree (DL) No 135/85 of 3 May 1985 ... 12, 36, 73
- art. 16 ... 36

Decree (DL) No 136/85 of 3 May 1985 ... 12, 36, 73
- art. 14 ... 36
- art. 15 ... 36
- art. 17 ... 36

Decree (DL) No 491/85 of 26 November 1985
- art. 8 ... 31, 49
- art. 48-50 ... 53

Decree (DL) No 38/87 of 23 December 1987
- art. 79 ... 51
- art. 83 ... 51

Decree (DL) No 154/88 of 29 April 1988 ... 12, 73

Decree (DL) No 426/88 of 18 November 1988 ... 11, 14, 19, 20, 21, 27, 30, 31, 37, 62, 64, 65

Decree (DL) No 426/88 (continued)
art. 9 38
art. 10 48
art. 11 50
art. 12 18
art. 13 64
art. 14 64
Decree (DL) No 969/88 of 15 December 1988 28
art. 70 28
Decree (DL) No 40/89 of 1 February 1989
Decree (DL) No 64-A/89 of 27 February 1989 ....16, 34-35
art. 9 ....16, 34
art. 12 34
art. 13 ....35, 49
art. 35 16
art. 8 21
Decree (DL) No 79-A/89 of 13 March 1989
art. 16 44
art. 36 44
Decree (DL) No 330/90 of 23 October 1990 12
art. 7 ....**79**
Decree (DL) No 166/91 of 9 May 1991 ....12, 77
art. 1 ....**77**
art. 2 53
art. 3 ....53, **77-78**
Decree (DRegul.) No 38/91 of 6 August 1991 ....7, 62
Decree (DL) No 440/91 of 14 November 1991 21
Decree (DL) No 451/91 of 4 December 1991 78
Decree (DL) No 235/92 of 24 October 1992 31

Ministerial Decrees

Ministerial Decree (P) No 186/73 of 13 March 1973 ....11, 20, 27, 36
art. 5 20
art. 8 20
Ministerial Decree (P) No 777/91 of 8 August 1991 ....12, 28
Ministerial Decree (P) No 1156/91 of 11 November 1991 28
Ministerial Decree (P) No 163/92 of 13 March 1992 28

Regulations etc.

Collective Agreement 1972
clause 22 85
Resolution No 22/85 of the Assembly of the Republic 62
Safety Regulations for the Mechanical Industry in Madeira
art. 78 89-92

TABLE OF CASES

[Numbers in bold type refer to pages at which extracts are printed verbatim]

Numerical Table of Cases before the Court of Justice of the European Communities

80/70 Defrenne *v.* Belgian State [1971] ECR 445 ... 42
43/75 Defrenne *v.* Sabena (No 2) [1976] ECR 455 ... 7
106/77 Amministrazione delle Finanze dello Stato *v.* Simmenthal SpA [1978] ECR 629 ... 9
149/77 Defrenne *v.* Sabena [1978] ECR 1365 ... 42
69/80 Worringham *v.* Lloyds Bank Ltd [1981] ECR 767 ... 42
152/84 Marshall *v.* Southampton and South-West Hampshire Area Health Authority [1986] ECR 723 ... 8, 43
C-345/89 Criminal proceedings against Stoeckel [1991] ECR I-4047 ... 76

Table of Cases: Constitutional Courts and Tribunals

Constitutional Commission,
20 July 1980 ... **93-97**
Constitutional Tribunal
20 May 1987 ... 97
18 November 1987 ... 97
20 September 1989 ... 98

Table of Cases: Supreme Court

24 October 1980 ... 85
4 June 1981 ... **82-84**

Table of Cases: Supreme Administrative Tribunal

27 February 1973 ... 81
22 May 1973 ... **81-82**
1 March 1990 ... 81

Table of Cases: Court of Appeal

Lisbon, 26 November 1979 ... **84-85**
Lisbon, 12 July 1982 ... **85**
Lisbon, 22 November 1982 ... 85, **86**
Lisbon, 12 October 1983 ... 86
Coimbra, 30 July 1986 ... 8
Coimbra, 8 March 1988 ... 27, **89-92**

Table of Cases: Labour Tribunal

Lisbon, 3 July 1990 ... 22, **86-88**

Alphabetical Table of Cases

Amministrazione delle Finanze dello Stato *v.* Simmenthal SpA, Case 106/77, [1978] ECR 629 (ECJ) 9
Caminhos de Ferro Portugueses EP *contra* Manuel Coutinho, *Ac. Doutr.*, No 343, July 1990, p. 1017 81
de Freitas Lopes, Manuel, e C^{a}, Ld^{a} *contra* Maria de Fátima Cunha, *Col. Jurisp.*, Coimbra, 13th year, Book II, 1988, p. 106 .... **89-92**
Defrenne *v.* Belgian State, Case 80/70, [1971] ECR 445 (ECJ) 42
Defrenne *v.* Sabena (No 2), Case 43/75, [1976] ECR 455 (ECJ) 7
Defrenne *v.* Sabena, Case 149/77, [1978] ECR 1365 (ECJ) 42
Estoril SARL *contra* Maria dos Anjos Vieira, *Ac. Doutr.*, No 140/141, August-September 1973, p. 1262 .... **81-82**
Estoril SARL *contra* Maria da Conceição Bráulio, *Ac. Doutr.*, No 235, July 1981, p. 954 .... **82-84**
Estoril SARL *contra* Maria Herminia Raposo, B.T.E., 2nd series, Nos 7-9, 1986, p. 1009 .... **85**
Estoril SARL *contra* Victória Maria Rodrigues, B.T.E., 2nd series, Nos 10-12, 1985, p. 1318 .... **86**
Estoril SARL *contra* Mariana de Oliveira, B.T.E., 2nd series, Nos 3-4, 1986, p. 384 86
Marshall *v.* Southampton and South-West Hampshire Area Health Authority, Case 152/84, [1986] ECR 723 (ECJ) 8, 43
Martins Rodrigues Pinto, Luisa *contra* Certifix, unreported **86-88**
Mota, Delfina Maria *contra* Estoril SARL, unreported 85
Public Ministry *contra* Portugal Previdente SARL, B.M.J., No 321, 1982, p. 231 .... **93-97**
Public Ministry *contra* Companhia de Seguros Tranquilidade EP, B.M.J., No 367, 1987, p. 273 97
Public Ministry *contra* Portugal Previdente SARL, D.R., 2nd series, No 41, 1988, p. 1622 97
Stoeckel, Criminal proceedings against, Case C-345/89, [1991] ECR I-4047 (ECJ) 76
Worringham *v.* Lloyds Bank Ltd, Case 69/80, [1981] ECR 767 (ECJ) 42

COMMENTARY ON

EQUALITY LAW

1. GENERAL

1.1 INTRODUCTION

1.1.1 INTRODUCTION TO THE NATIONAL LEGAL SYSTEM

The Portuguese Constitution of 2 April 1976, as subsequently amended, identifies the various sources of written law and stipulates the criteria of legal validity and effectiveness. The hierarchical structure of legal measures follows certain principles, notably those concerning the primacy of the law, and the equal force of laws and decrees. The expression 'primacy of the law' refers to the idea that the law prevails over all other State acts, particularly over those emanating from the executive power (such as regulations and administrative measures).

Three layers co-exist in Portugal's legal system: the State, the autonomous regions (the Azores and Madeira), and local government. This picture does not contradict the idea of a hierarchy of sources, but rather adds a horizontal dimension.

The system of constitutional review of legislative measures is mixed and complex. All tribunals (judicial, administrative, fiscal, military) may decide whether or not constitutional issues arise in a particular case. However, questions of constitutionality may also be settled by a body created especially for this purpose, the Constitutional Tribunal (*Tribunal Constitucional*). Moreover, the tribunals have direct access to the Constitution and may decide on the constitutionality of a measure.

Abstract and centralized review may be exercised by the Constitutional Tribunal before or after the coming into force of a law. It may be exercised when unconstitutionality results from an act or omission, even in the event of unconstitutional silence on the part of the legislative bodies.

Constitutional review is carried out not only on the basis of the written text of the Constitution, but also with reference to principles which may be implied from it. It is distinct from a review of legality; the latter occurs when the validity of legal measures is assessed in the light of other legislative provisions. For example, such control may focus on the legality of decrees (DL) in the light of the laws which authorized them.

Review of legality is exercised by tribunals of a judicial nature and by the Constitutional Tribunal, in cases where the conformity of a legislative standard is assessed in the context of laws of more significant force (such as organic laws). Review is exercised by the administrative tribunals when the illegality is the result of a violation of the law by legal measures which are inferior to it, or by individual and concrete administrative acts.

The first part of the Constitution deals essentially with fundamental rights. This part is not however exhaustive; other fundamental rights are provided for elsewhere in the Constitution, as well as in the rules of international law.[1] Moreover, art. 16(2) of the Constitution has its origin in the ratification of the Universal Declaration of Human Rights, passed by the General Assembly of the United Nations in New York on 10 December 1948. It elevates the principles of this Declaration to the status of Portuguese constitutional law. This provision thus places fundamental rights in a much larger context than the written Constitution, whilst anticipating the interpretation of the latter in light of the 1948 Declaration.

The principle of equality is described in general terms in art. 13 of the Constitution. It is then taken up again in several other provisions.

1.1.2 ECONOMIC AND SOCIAL CONTEXT

Although women constitute the majority of the electorate (52 per cent), they are a minority in the various organs of power. They played an active part in the process of democratization of the country and in the management of the new structures. During the revolution of 1974 they publicly expressed their views, something which the former régime had forbidden them to do. Many of them became aware of social injustices and declared themselves ready to intervene in the construction of a new society.

However, the new trends of opinion scarcely touched on women's affairs. The various trade union, civil and political organizations tended to leave positions with the least responsibility to women. For example, in 1991 the percentage of women members represented in the management bodies of trade union associations affiliated to the two central union groups was 17 per cent in the *Confederação Geral dos Trabalhadores Portugueses - Intersindical Nacional (C.G.T.P.-I.N.)* and 14 per cent in the *União Geral de Trabalhadores (U.G.T.)*. In the same way, and at the level of political structures, women are under-represented: there are scarcely 19 women out of 230 deputies in Parliament, 3 out of 24 deputies in the European Parliament, 7 out of 68 governmental posts, and there is not a single woman in the Council of State (*Conselho de Estado*).

In economic terms, women are becoming more and more numerous in the labour market. In fact, the rate of activity of women is increasing at a steady pace; it had reached 43.2 per cent by the end of 1990. The tendency to leave the labour market temporarily or permanently to carry out child-rearing responsibilities is becoming less frequent. This evolution reveals profound

---

1 Article 16(1) of the Constitution.

changes in society, especially at the family level. Thus the average number of children per woman decreased from 3 in 1970 to 1.5 in 1991.

However, many inequalities remain. Unemployment amongst women is higher than amongst men. This phenomenon results especially from the increased use of new technology, which tends to eliminate routine jobs; women are often employed in these types of jobs. Another observation is that part-time work mainly involves women (64 per cent in 1990).[1]

For a variety of reasons, equal pay for men and women is still far from being realized. Women's pay is still considered as complementing that of men. Women receive less in the way of benefits and bonuses (for attendance, productivity etc.), most notably due to the fact that they are absent more often, even where such absence is due to their responsibilities as mothers. Women work fewer hours, given that they are more likely to be in part-time work. Even if these differences in remuneration can also be seen in levels of qualification, these result especially from inequalities in training, in conditions for access to the professions and, generally, in working conditions (such as career development).

There is a visible segmentation of the labour market in Portugal, as there is elsewhere. Women are particularly to be found in employment where the qualification levels and remuneration are lowest. In the primary sector, women's work is concentrated in agriculture; in the secondary sector, it occurs mostly in the textile, clothing and shoe-making industries; in the tertiary sector, women are particularly found in commerce, various services, and in education.

The struggle for equality must therefore aim to integrate these two labour markets (male and female), and to bring about the changes in mentality which this implies. Various strategies may be envisaged. At State level, positive action, especially regarding professional training, would seem to be particularly appropriate. The structures for childcare should also be developed. Furthermore, as legislation is not sufficient to bring about access to complete equality, it is in the sphere of collective bargaining that measures should most urgently be taken; examples would include the granting of benefits to the family (rather than to women), or the adaptation of working hours to those of crèches or schools. At a family level, domestic responsibilities should be shared between partners, in order to place more value on the productivity of women's work.

---

1 We should, however, note two qualifications in relation to this statement: on the one hand, the rate of part-time work is particularly low in Portugal and, on the other hand, the rate of activity amongst women is particularly high.

1.2 SOURCES

1.2.1 INTERNATIONAL STANDARDS

1.2.1.1 Human rights

Article 8(1) of the Constitution is the result of the integration of international law into Portuguese law. International law is subject to the Constitution, but it takes precedence over normal domestic law. Therefore, national rules which are contrary to the principles of international law are void. This principle applies both to the general provisions of international law and to treaty provisions.

United Nations

Article 16(2) of the Constitution is the result of the formal acceptance of the Universal Declaration of Human Rights of 10 December 1948; it elevates its provisions to the status of constitutional principles. The Constitution must therefore be interpreted in light of the Declaration. Apart from principles common to the two texts, certain articles from the Declaration clarify doubts which had existed about certain constitutional standards and supply richer perspectives than can be obtained from domestic law.

The International Covenant on Civil and Political Rights and the International Covenant on Economic, Social and Cultural Rights of 16 December 1966 were ratified by Law No 29/78 of 12 June 1978 and by Law No 45/78 of 11 July 1978, respectively.

International Labour Organization (ILO)

Portugal has ratified 68 ILO conventions, some of which deal with the principle of equality.

Council of Europe

In Law No 65/78 of 13 October 1978, Portugal has ratified the European Convention on Human Rights and Fundamental Freedoms, signed in Rome on 4 November 1950.

1.2.1.2 Treaties on special questions

Portugal adopted the United Nations Covenant on the Elimination of All Forms of Discrimination against Women, signed in New York on 18 December 1979.[1] It has ratified all ILO conventions regarding matters of equality. The European Social Charter of the Council of Europe, signed in

1 Law No 23/80 of 26 June 1980.

Turin on 18 October 1961, was ratified by Decree (DRegul.) No 38/91 issued by the President of the Republic on 6 August 1991.

1.2.2 EUROPEAN COMMUNITY LAW

1.2.2.1 Direct effect of Community law

Article 8 of the Constitution provides for the general incorporation and for the full legal status of standards of international law in the domestic legal order. Included in this are the general rules of international law, as well as those arising under treaty provisions, and even those contained in secondary legislation. In fact, art. 8(3) provides that standards originating from competent organs of international organizations to which Portugal belongs will come directly into force within the domestic legal order if this is expressly stated in the establishing treaties in question.

This principle of direct applicability concerns provisions which, due to their nature and content, directly generate rights and obligations for persons who are subject to Portuguese law.

However, the question of direct applicability is closely linked to the primacy of international law in relation to domestic law. In order for it to be possible for an international law provision to be invoked within the domestic legal order, it must be possible for it to prevail over a provision of domestic law which is contrary to it. This primacy is provided for by the Constitution.

Portuguese rules relating to the primacy of international law also apply to European Community law. In this respect it is essential to take account of the case law of the European Court of Justice (ECJ) on the direct effect of EC law.

The provisions of treaties have direct effect, unless they quite clearly originate from a text or context which makes it impossible for them to have such an effect. Where there is a specific, unconditional and precise obligation (to do, or not to do, or to cease to do certain things), individuals may require observance of this obligation by the State before the national courts (direct vertical effect). Certain provisions may also create, for individuals, rights and obligations likely to be invoked before a court (direct horizontal effect).[1]

Secondary legislation does not have to be the subject of implementing measures in order to be integrated into domestic law in the Member States. In order to be applied by the judge, the substance should be presented in the form of a self-sufficient, unconditional and positive provision of law.

---

1 See art. 119 of the EEC Treaty, and *Defrenne* v. *Sabena*, Case 43/75, [1976] ECR 455 (ECJ).

It remains to be seen whether individuals may require the application of EC secondary legislation; the question of direct effect of the various sources has been settled by the ECJ.[1]

Regulations and Decisions in favour of individuals are directly effective. The same applies to Decisions in favour of a State where they impose a precise and unconditional obligation on the latter, without allowing it freedom of assessment and without requiring the adoption of a domestic legal provision in order to ensure full implementation. However, this type of Decision can only create rights affecting relations between Member States, and not between individuals (exclusion of direct horizontal effect). As far as Directives are concerned, the Court of Appeal (*Tribunal da Relação*) at Coimbra decided on 30 July 1986 that they 'may under certain conditions have direct effect, in such a way as to generate rights for individuals, likely to be invoked in their relations with the Member State in question (direct vertical effect)'.[2]

1.2.2.2 Retrospective implementation

The primacy of EC law over prior or subsequent domestic law does not pose a problem. In fact, art. 8 of the Constitution provides that the principles and standards of international law prevail over ordinary domestic law, in accordance with international jurisprudence. This ensures the unity and coherence of the hierarchy of sources of law as provided for in the Constitution.[3]

However, the Constitution very clearly imposes its primacy over all other law, including international law. Article 277(1) of the Constitution stipulates that standards which violate the provisions of the Constitution or the principles contained in it are unconstitutional. Similarly, art. 207(1) prohibits courts from applying such standards.

In order to guarantee this primacy, the Constitution set up a system of review of constitutionality which is preventative and *a posteriori*. Preventative review of treaties and international agreements, which has been entrusted to the Constitutional Tribunal, is not obligatory. On the other hand, Parliament can by a majority vote decide not to take account of a decision of unconstitutionality. International rules in force in the domestic legal order may also be subject to *a posteriori* review: tribunals under the control of the Constitutional Tribunal may apply no standard which is contrary to the Constitution, even if it originates from an international convention.[4] This

---

1 *Marshall* v. *Southampton and South-West Hampshire Area Health Authority*, Case 152/84, [1986] ECR 723 (ECJ).

2 Quoted by J. MOTA DE CAMPOS, *Direito Comunitario*, 1990, Lisbon, No 816, p. 269.

3 See §1.1.1 above.

4 Article 280(3) of the Constitution.

system is incompatible with the principles of international law, developed in particular in the Vienna Convention of 23 May 1969.

The system of constitutional review may obviously pose problems in the context of the need to ensure the primacy of EC law. Although Portugal, by signing the Treaty of Accession for Portugal's membership of the European Community on 12 June 1985, undertook to respect the primacy of EC law, the latter is itself subject to constitutional review.[1] It is thus conceivable that a Community standard could be declared unconstitutional in Portugal. This would constitute an infringement of a fundamental principle of EC law, as contained in the *Simmenthal* decision of 9 March 1978.[2] However, the probability of such an eventuality occurring is small, primarily due to the constitutional revision of 1982, which removed discrepancies between the two legal orders.

1.2.3 CONSTITUTIONAL LAW

The current Constitution of the Republic of Portugal of 2 April 1976 has been revised twice, first in 1982 and again in 1989.

In spite of the absence of a specific provision on equality between the sexes in all spheres, the Constitution gives certain guarantees in this respect (in particular the prohibition of discrimination and the protection of maternity), and it suggests various courses of action (including legislative and executive action). Article 81 classifies as a priority for the State the responsibility for promoting the improvement of social and economic well-being, as well as of the quality of life for the people, particularly that of the least favoured classes.[3] The State must also ensure full use of the powers of production.[4] In a democratic system this provision obviously includes women.

Article 13(2) contains the principle of non-discrimination based on sex. It is a general rule which has a residual character for matters which are not dealt with by their own provisions (in political matters) or which are only dealt with in an incomplete way (in family matters).

The Constitution has deliberately tended towards the prohibition of discrimination based on sex in two major spheres. First, equality in the family abolishes all domination of the husband over his wife;[5] secondly, equality of opportunity[6] and of working conditions are confirmed.[7]

---

1 *Ibid.*

2 *Amministrazione delle Finanze dello Stato* v. *Simmenthal SpA*, Case 106/77, [1978] ECR 629 (ECJ).

3 Article 81(a) of the Constitution.

4 Article 81(c) of the Constitution.

5 Article 36 of the Constitution.

6 This includes training: see art. 74 of the Constitution.

7 Articles 47, 48 and 59 of the Constitution.

In several articles the Constitution deals with the protection of maternity. We should note that since 1982 the importance of paternity has been recognized at the same level as maternity. Maternity and paternity are of great social value, as they represent a major investment for society. The State should, therefore, take steps to avoid the participation of mothers and fathers in professional life and in civic life being affected by this investment.[1] The State therefore has the responsibility of taking steps to protect the family, such as the creation of infrastructures for supporting the family.[2] Moreover, women who work receive special protection during and after pregnancy.

1.2.4 LEGISLATION

1.2.4.1 Prior legislation

The principle of 'equal pay for equal work' was provided for in art. 116 of Decree (DL) No 49408 of 24 November 1969. Article 118 of this decree gave women the right not to have to carry out tasks which were medically unsuitable during pregnancy and up to three months following pregnancy, the right not to be dismissed without just cause during pregnancy and for one year after childbirth, the right to maternity leave of 60 days, as well as the right to interrupt work in order to breastfeed their child. Article 119 of the same decree provided that access by women to all professions, jobs or work could only be restricted in order to protect their health or to protect their family. Finally, art. 120 imposed on companies and the State the task of creating working conditions (such as part-time work and the setting up of crèches) which are best suited to the needs of the woman worker with family responsibilities.

Decree (DL) No 112/76 of 7 February 1976 extended the period of maternity leave to 90 days.

Until recently the sphere of social security contained much discrimination. Thus the concept of head of family, used in particular to give access to family benefits, was maintained for a long time. Also, a difference between the contributions payable by male and female agricultural workers led to effects on the benefits which were available to them respectively.

Article 23 of Decree (DL) No 303/83 of 28 June 1983 attempted to establish equality in advertising. According to this provision, 'advertising shall not convey the idea of the inferiority or subordination of women in relation to men or reduce them to a domestic role, by over-valuing it to the detriment of other functions or aspirations'. This text also declared unlawful 'advertising which uses the image of the woman as a simple promotional object for goods or services of which she is not the exclusive consumer'. This

1 Article 68(1) of the Constitution.
2 Article 67 of the Constitution.

law was revised, but in its new, more vague, form it runs the risk of being less effective.[1]

The Civil Code of 1966, inherited from the former political régime, maintained a system where the husband was superior and was considered to be the head of the family. It was therefore incumbent on him to choose the family home, to administer household assets and to exercise paternal power. Furthermore, he could intervene in the contract of employment drawn up for his wife. The latter found herself confined to the administration of domestic assets placed under her charge. This scheme was repealed by the Constitution of 1976.

Decree (DL) No 485/77 of 17 November 1977 set up the Commission for the Female Condition (*Commissão da Condição Feminina*). This was later restructured, due primarily to the achievement of previous objectives and thus the development of new objectives.

1.2.4.2 Present legislation

Current legislation in Portugal in matters of equality is fairly comprehensive. Equal pay and equal treatment in the private sector were provided for in Decree (DL) No 392/79 of 20 September 1979. Decree (DL) No 426/88 of 18 November 1988 extended these principles to workers in public administration.

This represents an advance in comparison with the Constitution of 1976, which only provided for non-discrimination. Today positive action is expressly permitted by the Decree.[2] The Commission for Equality in Work and in Employment (*Comissão para a Igualdade no Trabalho e no Emprego*) was constituted within the Ministry of Employment and Social Security (*Ministério do Emprego e da Segurança Social*).

Equal pay is provided for, both as a matter of principle and in matters of implementation. Provisions contrary to it are null and void.

Equal access, equal opportunities (especially concerning professional training and career development) and equal treatment in general are established by law. Article 8 of Decree (DL) No 392/79 of 20 September 1979 provided for the prohibition of certain work which could be dangerous for women, or subjected these jobs to various conditions protecting women. Ministerial Decree (P) No 186/73 of 13 March 1973 relating to these matters is still in force. Night work by women is expressly prohibited by Decree (DL) No 409/71 of 27 September 1971. However, these provisions should be considered as abrogated, and legal proceedings can be brought to establish the invalidity of discriminatory rules.

---

1 See §1.2.4.2 below.

2 Article 3(2) of Decree (DL) No 392/79 of 20 September 1979.

Law No 4/84 of 5 April 1984 governs maternity and paternity, particularly leave, absence from work for consultations and breastfeeding, longer absences, the arrangement of work schedules in special circumstances, inadvisable tasks and subsidies. Decrees (DL) No 135/85 and No 136/85 of 3 May 1985 fixed the methods of implementation of this law in the public and private sectors respectively. Decree (DL) No 154/88 of 29 April 1988 completed Decree (DL) No 136/85.

Inequalities in social security matters have been abolished. All that remains is the difference in retirement age in the private sector.[1]

Law No 30/87 of 7 July 1987 introduced the possibility of women being able to enrol in the army under conditions which were to be defined subsequently. Ministerial Decree (P) No 777/91 of 8 August 1991 then allowed women to complete their actual military service within the air force, in certain categories of jobs and specialized sections.

Decree (DL) No 330/90 of 23 October 1990, instituting the new advertising code, simply prohibited advertising which undermined the dignity of human beings and which contained discrimination based on sex. This very general law would seem to be less effective in matters of equality than the law which it replaced.[2]

Decree (DL) No 496/77 of 25 November 1977 adapted the Civil Code to the new Constitution of 1976. Following a comparative study with a view to bringing Portuguese law into line with other European laws, the legislature proceeded with an in-depth revision of the legal framework dealing with marriage and parenthood. Equality of rights and obligations between a married couple was also established. Each of the partners could carry out any profession or activity without the consent of the other.

Decree (DL) No 166/91 of 9 May 1991 created the Commission for Equality and for Women's Rights (*Comissão para a Igualdade e para Direitos das Mulheres*), which replaced the Commission for the Female Condition (CCF). The legislature wanted to embark on a new phase, given that some of the objectives conferred on the CCF had been achieved (such as equality before the law). It was advisable however to maintain the efforts with a view to achieving equality in practice and the change in attitude which it required. It was with this aim that the objectives and the structure of the Commission were reorganized.

Under Decrees (DL) No 251/74 of 12 June 1974, No 308/74 of 6 July 1974 and No 492/74 of 27 September 1974, access for women to careers in local administration, diplomatic work and the judiciary was made possible.

---

1 Decree (DRegul.) No 45266 of 23 September 1963.

2 See §1.2.4.1.above.

2. BASIC CONCEPTS

2.1 THE CONCEPTS OF EQUALITY AND DISCRIMINATION

Article 13 of the Constitution provides for the equality of citizens. This is a legal provision which applies to individuals, corporate bodies and groups. This principle of equality has to be respected not only in relationships between citizens and the State, but also within institutions, associations or groups.

The principle of equality can be said to have three dimensions:[1]

(a) the prohibition of arbitrary conduct: any unequal treatment without reasonable justification based on objective criteria, as well as equal treatment in different situations, is unlawful;
(b) the prohibition of discrimination: any differentiation in the treatment of citizens based on purely subjective categories is unlawful;[2]
(c) the obligation to differentiate in order to compensate for inequality of opportunities: this entails the elimination by the public authorities of actual inequalities of a social, economic or cultural nature.[3]

The result of this analysis is that equality both in law and in fact is to be ensured. Equality in practice complements formal equality in the event of the latter masking a social inequality.

Apart from art. 13 of the Constitution, legal equality is secured most particularly in relation to certain special rights: equality of spouses,[4] equality of opportunity regarding the choice of profession or type of work,[5] equal pay for equal work,[6] as well as the protection of maternity and paternity.[7]

Real equality can justify positive discrimination. This may take the form, for example, of special protection for a certain group of citizens. The application of a more favourable framework is however temporary in nature, given that its legitimacy rests on a combination of circumstances which are to be overcome.[8]

---

1 J. J. GOMES CANOTILHO and M. VITAL MOREIRA, *Constituiçao da República Portuguesa Anotada*, 1991, Coimbra, p. 147.
2 See art. 13(2) of the Constitution.
3 See arts 9(d), 58(3)(b) and 74(1) of the Constitution.
4 Article 36(2) of the Constitution.
5 Article 58(3)(b) of the Constitution.
6 Article 59(1)(a) of the Constitution.
7 Article 68 of the Constitution.
8 See also J. MIRANDA, *Manuel de Direito Constitucional,* 1988, Coimbra, Book IV, p. 233.

Article 2(a) of Decree (DL) No 392/79 of 20 September 1979 has defined discrimination as:

> Any distinction, exclusion, restriction or preference based on sex, which has as its aim or result to compromise or refuse to recognize the enjoyment or the exercise of rights guaranteed by employment legislation.

This legislation, which applies the private sector, is called the 'equality law'. It has been extended to the public sector by Decree (DL) No 426/88 of 18 November 1988.

2.2 DIRECT DISCRIMINATION

2.2.1 DEFINITION

Article 3(1) of Decree (DL) No 392/79 of 20 September 1979 prohibits direct or indirect discrimination, especially with reference to marital status or family status. This provision does not contain a definition of direct discrimination, but it is possible to deduce certain elements of this by reading it alongside art. 2(a).

2.2.1.1 Reason

According to art. 2(a), discrimination consists of any distinction, restriction or preference based on sex whose aim or consequence is to compromise or to refuse to acknowledge the enjoyment or exercise of rights ensured by employment legislation. It is possible to deduce from this that a finding of discrimination does not necessarily require an intention to discriminate.

2.2.1.2 Detriment

The victim of direct discrimination has the onus of establishing the facts. Compensation for any damage suffered by the victim is governed by law. Decree (DL) No 392/79 of 20 September 1979 contains provisions on this subject.[1]

A distinction is made according to whether compensation is due because of a violation of the equal pay or of the equal treatment principle. In the event of unequal pay, case law grants the difference in salary for the months for which it is due and orders the remuneration paid to women to be replaced by that paid to men, in application of art. 12(2) of Decree (DL) No 392/79 of 20 September 1979. In unequal treatment cases, the most common means of

1 Articles 11, 12 and 16.

redress is compensation. If there has been an improper dismissal, reinstatement of the worker may be sought.[1]

2.2.1.3 Comparator

No comparator is required in cases involving access to employment. In equal treatment cases comparisons are made within a single undertaking.

2.2.2 EXTENDED DEFINITION

2.2.2.1 Marital status

Reference to marital status may not in law be a basis of discrimination.[2] In practice, however, it is common , particularly in recruitment.

2.2.2.2 Family status

The situation described regarding marital status is also true, *mutatis mutandis,* of family status.

2.2.2.3 Pregnancy

During procedures for hiring employees, the candidate need not supply information regarding pregnancy. Different treatment of a candidate due to pregnancy amounts to discrimination.

2.2.2.4 Sexual harassment

Sexual harassment is a reality in the Portuguese labour market. Women are becoming increasingly aware of this discrimination and are seeking to assert their rights. It is possible to bring a complaint before the Commission for Equality in Work and in Employment, but there is no specific legal protection. Depending on the case, employment legislation, criminal law, or even both can be applied. The victim of dismissal or of any improper disciplinary action,[3] including victimization, can go either to the union to seek representation before a tribunal, or to the Public Ministry. The victim of any insult or sexual offence may bring a complaint to the police.

Article 21(1) of Decree (DL) No 49408 of 24 November 1969 provides that the employer may not transfer a female worker to another work site, except in cases provided for by law.[4] Article 40 of this Decree obliges the employer to ensure that work is carried out in conditions of discipline, safety,

---

1 See §4.9 below.
2 See art. 3(1) of Decree (DL) No 392/79 of 20 September 1979.
3 See §4.9 below.
4 Article 21(1)(e).

hygiene, and morality. It then obliges him to discipline any person who, through his or her conduct, provokes or creates conditions of demoralization amongst workers, especially amongst women.

Decree (DL) No 64-A/89 of 27 February 1989 allows a female worker to terminate her contract of employment where she has suffered abusive conditions or legally punishable infringements on her physical integrity, her freedom, her honour or her dignity caused by the employer or his representatives.[1] Article 9(2) of this Decree provides that the employer must apply disciplinary sanctions against any person who violates the rights and guarantees applying to workers in a company[2] or who, within the company, commits acts of physical, abusive or offensive violence punishable by law against workers in the enterprise.[3]

2.2.2.5 Physical attributes

Article 7(2) of Decree (DL) No 392/79 of 20 September 1979 provides:

> Recruitment for any position shall be based exclusively on objective criteria, and the formulation of physical requirements which have no bearing on the professions or the conditions under which they are exercised shall be prohibited.

2.2.2.6 Dress codes

There are no dress codes for workers in Portuguese law, at least at a general level.

2.3 INDIRECT DISCRIMINATION

2.3.1 DEFINITION

The law contains no definition of the concept of indirect discrimination. Given the difficulty in defining the concept, in Portugal as in other countries in the European Community, clarification can be sought from reports drawn up within the scope of the Network of Experts on the Implementation of the Equality Directives, especially the Consolidated Report of 1987.[4] In this it was suggested that indirect discrimination consisted of three constituent elements: a condition or requirement for a job, which was neither essential nor objectively justifiable, and which would have a disproportionate and adverse impact on members of one sex or a particular marital status. Indirect discrimination is prohibited in all areas covered by the Directives. In

---

1 Article 35(1)(c) and (f).

2 Article 9(2)(b).

3 Article 9(2)(i).

4 F. VON PRONDZYNSKI, *Implementation of the Equality Directives*, 1987, Commission of the European Communities, Luxembourg.

practice, however, the legal provisions are not consistently applied, and instances of indirect discrimination remain numerous in Portugal.

2.3.2 SUSPECT CRITERIA

Hours of work

The prohibition of night-work for women[1] may be considered as having been abolished.[2] In fact, given that women's access to day or night work may not be prohibited or subjected to conditions, except for the reasons stated in art. 8 of Decree (DL) No 392/79 of 20 September 1979, the prohibition of night-work should be considered as repealed. Case law has moreover decided that it was discriminatory where the prohibition of night-work for women prevented them from being paid higher wages.[3]

Decree (DL) No 421/83 of 2 December 1983 on overtime exempts pregnant women or women with children of less than 10 months from the obligation to work overtime.[4]

Marital status

Under art. 3(1) of Decree (DL) No 392/79, reference to marital status must not be a source of either direct or indirect discrimination.[5]

2.3.3 DISPROPORTIONATE IMPACT

The hiring of staff by the *Banco Comercial Português* has provided an illustration of the disproportionate impact which certain unjustifiable requirements may have. The bank recruited almost only men, on the pretext that each employee was required to prove total availability for work. This practice implied that household and family-related tasks are the responsibility of women. It removed from women the equality of opportunity to which they are entitled.[6]

Segmentation of the labour market is a significant phenomenon in Portugal. To our knowledge, there is however no case law analyzing this phenomenon in the context of the concept of indirect discrimination.

---

1 Article 31 of Decree (DL) No 409/71 of 27 September 1971.

2 See arts 13 and 58(3)(b) of the Constitution and arts 3, 4(2), 8 and 23 of Decree (DL) No 392/79, of 20 September 1979.

3 See §1.2.4.2 above, and §§3.7.3 and 4.14.1.3 below.

4 Article 3(2)(b).

5 See §2.2.2.1 above.

6 See *Pareceres da Comissão para a Igualdade no Trabalho e no Emprego*, p. 68.

2.3.4 OBJECTIVE JUSTIFICATION

Apart from art. 7(2) of Decree (DL) No 392/79 of 20 September 1979,[1] no legislative text provides for objective justification for conditions the effect of which would be to exclude women from certain jobs.

2.4 VICTIMIZATION

Employers may neither prevent their workers from exercising their rights, nor dismiss them or apply penalties for this reason.[2] They may not reduce their pay or lower their professional classification in circumstances other than those instances provided for by law.[3] This rule applies to sex-based discrimination.[4]

1 See §2.2.2.5 above.

2 Article 21(1)(a) of Decree (DL) No 49408 of 24 November 1969.

3 See art. 21(1)(c) and (d).

4 See art. 11 of Decree (DL) No 392/79 of 20 September 1979, and art. 12 of Decree (DL) No 426/88 of 18 November 1988.

3. EQUAL PAY

3.1 PRINCIPLE

The equal pay principle is contained in art. 59(1) of the Constitution:

> All workers, without distinction as to age, sex, race, citizenship, country of origin, religion, political or ideological convictions, shall have the right to:
> (a) remuneration for work, in accordance with its quantity, nature and quality, applying the principle of 'equal pay for equal work', in such a way as to guarantee a minimum standard of living; ... .

It is repeated in art. 9(1) of Decree (DL) No 392/79 of 20 September 1979, which provides for the obligation to pay the same remuneration for equal work or for work of equal value. Decree (DL) No 426/88 of 18 November 1988 extended this principle to the public sector.

3.2 EXCEPTIONS

3.2.1 SIZE

All discrimination based on sex is prohibited, whatever the size of the enterprise. Any difference in remuneration resulting from this is therefore also unlawful, whatever the size of the company.

3.2.2 WORK DONE OUTSIDE THE JURISDICTION

The rules of private international law determine the proper law applicable to a particular employment relationship. The principle of equality should be applied in all instances where Portuguese law governs the case.

As far as the autonomous regions are concerned (the Azores and Madeira), Decrees (DL) No 392/79 of 20 September 1979 and No 426/88 of 18 November 1988 also apply. Article 21 of Decree (DL) No 392/79, however, provides that it is incumbent on the governments of the autonomous regions 'to proceed with the creation, at regional level, of structures which are adequate for the achievement of the objectives of the present law, as well as to propose the forms of statements with the *Comissão para a Igualdade no Trabalho e no Emprego* provided for in article 14 and with the representatives of the Labour Inspectorate'.

3.2.3 HEALTH AND SAFETY

Article 8(1) of Decree (DL) No 392/79 of 20 September 1979 provides that work considered by law as carrying actual or potential risks to health is prohibited or subject to certain conditions. Although para. 2 of this provision provides for periodic revision, Ministerial Decree (P) No 186/73 of 13 March 1973 still governs this matter. This text contains prohibitions aimed, on the one hand, at women in general, and on the other hand at pregnant women. It is clearly specified in the Decree, however, that women workers who have to cease carrying out their chosen work may not receive remuneration below that granted to them before ceasing the work.[1]

3.2.4 NATIONAL SECURITY

The principle of equal pay should be applied without any restrictions in the context of national security, in accordance with Decree (DL) No 426/88 of 18 November 1988.

3.2.5 RELIGION, RELIGIOUS SCHOOLS

The concept of an 'employer' includes 'any individual or corporate body who has the power, in their capacity as an employer, to conclude individual employment contracts'.[2] The principle applies also to Church schools.

3.2.6 RETIREMENT AGE

Retirement age is relevant to equal treatment. Pensions not being considered as remuneration under Portuguese law, this question will not be considered in the present section.

3.3 PERSONAL SCOPE OF PRINCIPLE

3.3.1 EMPLOYEES

Decree (DL) No 392/79 of 20 September 1979 applies to workers who have an individual contract of employment,[3] as well as to apprentices.[4]

3.3.2 INDEPENDENT CONTRACTORS

The above-mentioned Decree may be interpreted, *a contrario,* as not affecting self-employed workers. However, the constitutional principle of non-discrimination remains applicable with respect to these persons.

---

1 Articles 5 and 8 of the Ministerial Decree.

2 Article 2(b) of Decree (DL) No 392/79 of 20 September 1979.

3 *Ibid.*

4 Article 13.

3.3.3 HOME WORKERS

Article 20(1) of Decree (DL) No 392/79 of 20 September 1979 provides that the position of home workers is governed by an autonomous scheme, which may contain differences imposed by the specific nature of this sector. Decree (DL) No 440/91 of 14 November 1991 regulates home work. Given that this text does not provide for any derogation from the principle of equal pay, it is appropriate to consider Decree (DL) No 392/79 as applying to this category of workers.

3.3.4 PUBLIC SECTOR

In application of art. 20(2) of Decree (DL) No 392/79 of 20 September 1979, Decree (DL) No 426/88 of 18 November 1988 extends the principle of equal pay to workers employed in public administration.

3.3.5 DOMESTIC EMPLOYEES

This concept occurs in employment law as well as in social security law. Persons employed in private homes are covered by the principle of equal pay. Housewives are not considered as workers in the sense of the law, unless they have a contract of employment. Nevertheless, they may take out voluntary national insurance.[1] This is a matter for social security.

3.3.6 NON-EMPLOYED POPULATION

The principle does not apply to the non-employed population (such as the unemployed).

3.4 ACTIVITIES COVERED

Article 2(b) of Decree (DL) No 392/79 of 20 September 1979 is directed at 'all employers'. In principle, all remuneration for an activity carried out in the scope of a contract of employment or in the public sector is covered by the principle of equality.

3.5 DEFINITION OF REMUNERATION

3.5.1 ARTICLE 119 OF THE EEC TREATY

The definition in art. 119 of the EEC Treaty is repeated in art. 2(c) of Decree (DL) No 392/79 of 20 September 1979. The latter lists examples of the various elements of remuneration.

---

1 Article 8 of Decree (DL) No 40/89 of 1 February 1989.

3.5.2 FRINGE BENEFITS

Article 2(c) of Decree (DL) No 392/79 of 20 September 1979 contains a list of examples of fringe benefits which may be considered as constituting remuneration.[1] Article 82 of Decree (DL) No 49408 of 24 November 1969 also defines the concept of remuneration: it includes 'basic remuneration and all other regular or periodic payments made, directly or indirectly, in money or cash'. Article 88 defines the notion of bonus: it only constitutes remuneration if it is due under a contract or rules governing it, or if it is as a matter of custom of importance and is of a regular and permanent nature. For example, an attendance bonus which is paid regularly and is of a permanent nature can be considered part of the remuneration.

It should be noted that in practice the increasing use of fringe benefits, such as a bonus for attendance or for productivity, provides opportunities for discrimination. In fact, these bonuses are often denied to women when they have to be absent or to cease working for family or maternity reasons.

3.5.3 CONTRIBUTIONS BY EMPLOYER

Contributions paid by the employer in the context of the legal social security system do not constitute part of remuneration. On the other hand, contributions to complementary insurance schemes could be considered as remuneration.

3.5.4 CONTRIBUTIONS BY EMPLOYEE

Any contribution paid by workers, whether it is within the scope of the statutory social security system or is paid under complementary schemes, is an integral part of remuneration.

3.5.5 POST-CONTRIBUTION BENEFITS

Payments made for sickness, death etc. do not constitute remuneration.

Neither the amounts paid following termination of a contract of employment, nor damages paid in the event of a breach of the contract, constitute remuneration.

3.5.6 PENSIONS

Legal or complementary pensions belong in the area of social security and do not constitute remuneration.

3.5.7 COLLECTIVE AGREEMENTS

Portuguese law contains no information on this subject.

---

1 Lisbon labour tribunal, 3 July 1990.

3.6 COMPARATOR

3.6.1 SAME ESTABLISHMENT

Regarding the application of rules on equality, the comparison should be made in relation to the same single employer.

3.6.2 CONTEMPORANEOUS EMPLOYMENT

Regarding the implementation of the principle of equal pay, it is possible to compare pay due for simultaneous work.

3.6.3 HYPOTHETICAL MALE

Portuguese law contains no information on this subject.

3.6.4 DIFFERENT ESTABLISHMENT/SAME EMPLOYER

Comparisons in relation to the principle of equal pay are made in relation to one single employer only.

3.6.5 CROSS-INDUSTRY COMPARISONS

In Portugal, this type of comparison is only made for certain surveys. These have most notably found that it is those sectors made up mostly of women where remuneration is the lowest.

3.7 WOMAN DOES SAME WORK AS MAN

3.7.1 IDENTICAL WORK

Article 9(1) of Decree (DL) No 392/79 of 20 September 1979 provides for equal pay for equal work, for a job which implies the performance of equal tasks or tasks of an equal nature.

3.7.2 SIMILAR WORK

Article 9(1) also extends the principle of equal pay for equal work to work of equal value, which is performed for the same employer and where the component tasks, although of a different nature, are considered as equivalent through the application of an objective evaluation of the constituent aspects. It should be noted that the artificial establishment of various functions within the same job category, resulting in discrimination, constitutes a breach of the principle of equality.

3.7.3 NIGHT-WORK

The prohibition of night-work for women, contained in arts 31 and 32 of Decree (DL) No 409/71 of 27 September 1971, should perhaps be considered as abolished. It is not permitted to discriminate in this context.[1]

3.8 EQUAL VALUE

3.8.1 JOB EVALUATION

Article 9(3) of Decree (DL) No 392/79 of 20 September 1979 provides that 'systems for describing tasks and the evaluation of functions must rest on certain objective criteria common to men and to women, in such a way as to exclude all discrimination based on sex'.

3.8.2 JOB CLASSIFICATION

3.8.2.1 Factors

Professional classification is set up in a collective agreement or by ministerial decree, with reference to the 'National Classification of Professions', which provides for categories of tasks.

The social partners are free to organize tasks and categories in accordance with the specific nature of the sector. In practice, the content is approximately the same in all agreements.

3.8.2.2 Weightings

The categories fixed according to tasks are sub-divided into grades, either within the company (in company agreements), or for an entire industrial sector (in collective agreements).

3.8.2.3 Traditional male/female

The segmentation of the labour market in Portugal leads to differences in remuneration paid in the 'female' and the 'male' sectors. This is the result of various factors, such as the assumption that women are less productive than men, or the differences in the training of men and women which, initially, will determine employment options. These frequently have their origin in approaches and attitudes in areas such as careers guidance in schools. More generally, they lead to a view of women's role in society, which in turn influences the organs of power.[2]

---

1 See §1.2.4.2 above.

2 See §1.1.2 above.

There are, therefore, traditional 'female' and 'male' professions. Women are strongly represented in the scientific and liberal professions, which can in part be explained by their activity in certain public service sectors, particularly teaching. In 1990, the rate of female participation in the public service was 53.7 per cent, 15.9 per cent of which relates to management personnel and 35 per cent to higher-ranking technical staff.

3.8.3 HIGHER VALUE

Portuguese law contains no information on this subject.

3.8.4 PROPORTIONATE PAY

The principle of 'equal pay for equal work' contained in Portuguese law implies that there is an entitlement to proportionate pay in appropriate cases.

3.9 LEGITIMATE REASON FOR PAY DIFFERENTIAL

3.9.1 MATERIAL DIFFERENCE

If tasks which are different are nevertheless equivalent according to objective criteria, there is work of equal value leading to an entitlement to equal pay. If this is not so, a difference in pay may be justified.

3.9.2 ECONOMIC BENEFITS/MARKET FORCES

Portuguese law contains no information on this subject.

3.9.3 NIGHT-WORK

At the present time, the prohibition of night-work and its consequences in remuneration are no longer legal.[1] This is the position under case law.

3.9.4 PART-TIME WORK

In the case of part-time work, remuneration must correspond, at least proportionately, to the time devoted to the work. Thus, Decree (DL) No 167/80 of 20 May 1980 provides in art. 3 that half the remuneration is due for part-time work in public administration. For the private sector, art. 43 of Decree (DL) No 409/71 of 27 September 1971 regulates part-time work: collective agreements must contain rules relating to part-time work; they must facilitate access to part-time work for women with family responsibilities; remuneration may not be less than the proportion of full-

---

1 See §§1.2.4.2 and 3.7.3 above, and §4.14.1.3 below.

time remuneration corresponding to the work carried out. This principle is repeated in art. 20 of Law No 4/84 of 5 April 1984 on maternity.

Women are, in practice, the main participants in part-time work.[1]

3.9.5 RED CIRCLES

The law fixes a minimum rate of pay which sets a lower limit which must be observed in pay-fixing instruments. More often than not, women are paid the minimum rates.

Pay is fixed according to branch or sector through a collective instrument of regulation and as a function of professional categories. Within the undertaking, there is a sub-division into grades, where pay may not be less for different professional categories than that prescribed in the collective instruments of regulation of employment.

3.10 LEVELLING UP/DOWN

Article 12(2) of Decree (DL) No 392/79 of 20 September 1979 provides for the principle of equalizing pay upwards. Where there is a finding of unequal pay, the remuneration paid to men must in law replace that paid to women.

1 See however p. 5, footnote 1, above.

4. EQUAL TREATMENT

4.1 PRINCIPLE

The principle of equality treatment is guaranteed by Decree (DL) No 392/79 of 20 September 1979, which applies to the private sector and which was extended to the public sector by Decree (DL) No 426/88 of 18 November 1988. The nature and field of application of the principle are also specified in these texts. This principle applies to the relationship between employers and employees, as well as to those between employees.

4.2 EXCEPTIONS

4.2.1 EXCLUSIONS

4.2.1.1 Size

The principle of equal treatment applies to all undertakings, whatever their size.

4.2.1.2 Work done outside the jurisdiction

Where Portuguese law is declared as applicable to a situation under the principles of private international law, the principle of equal treatment will apply.

4.2.1.3 Health and safety

Exceptions justified for reasons of health and safety are provided for in art. 8 of Decree (DL) No 392/79 of 20 September 1979. Ministerial Decree (P) No 186/73 of 13 March 1973 contains the list of jobs prohibited to women. Furthermore, certain tasks are prohibited for pregnant women.[1]

4.2.1.4 National security

Article 276(1) of the Constitution provides that 'the defence of the homeland is a right and a fundamental duty of all Portuguese people'. Article 2 of the Constitution adds that 'military service is obligatory, within the terms and for the period which the law shall prescribe'.

Law No 29/82 of 1 December 1982 relating to national defence and to the armed forces confirms the obligation of citizens to contribute to national

---

1 Coimbra court of appeal, 8 March 1988.

defence.[1] Law No 30/87 of 7 July 1987 relating to military service reaffirms this principle in art. 1, and provides in art. 40 that women are exempt from military service; they may, however, carry out voluntary military service within the limits set out in special rules. The methods of application of this Law, set out in Decree (DL) No 969/88 of 15 December 1988, specify that women already in service have the right to have their situation maintained; their career will continue to comply with the statutory regime applicable (art. 70 of the decree).

Ministerial Decree (P) No 777/91 of 8 August 1991 authorizes the voluntary application by women, under conditions equal to those applying to men, for actual military service within the air force, in two categories of jobs and special services.

Ministerial Decree (P) No 1156/91 of 11 November 1991 allows women to enrol voluntarily in the army (actual military service), under equal conditions as those applying to men. Ministerial Decree (P) No 163/92 of 13 March 1992 extends this possibility to the navy.

It may be concluded from this legislation that access by women to positions in the army, despite the fact that it has been greatly reformed over the last few years, is not entirely equal to that applying to men. It should nevertheless be stressed that, after her entry into the army, a woman may not receive unfavourable treatment in the development of her career.[2]

The conditions of access to jobs within the police force take account of differences in aptitude in order to allow full access for women.

4.2.1.5 Religion, religious schools

Article 2(b) of Decree (DL) No 392/79 of 20 September 1979 applies to all employer bodies capable of concluding a contract of employment. Consequently, church schools are included in the field of application of the law.

4.2.1.6 Retirement age

This is a social security issue.

4.2.2 SEX AS A DETERMINING FACTOR

4.2.2.1 Lists

Article 7(3) of Decree (DL) No 392/79 of 20 September 1979 provides that reserving a job for one sex in work related to fashion, art or the theatre is not discriminatory where the nature of the task justifies this. This principle

1 Article 9(2) of the Law.
2 Article 28(3) of Law No 29/82 of 1 December 1982.

applies also to the public sector. However, the legislature has not drawn up a list enumerating the relevant professions in a more specific way. Where necessary, tribunals will have to decide on this subject.

4.2.2.2 Genuine occupational qualification

The main source of segmentation of the labour market lies in the stereotypes used by the population, which influence education and professional training choices. Women are thus led to opt for educational choices which distance them from certain professions.[1] Moreover, once inside the labour market, women suffer discrimination in access to professional training and promotion, which prevents them from obtaining posts requiring higher qualifications and management positions.

Thus, in 1990, men filled 61.9 per cent of salaried positions, 83.1 per cent of senior executive positions, 75.2 per cent of middle ranking executive positions, 82.1 per cent of team manager positions, 65.3 per cent of highly qualified staff and 67.7 per cent of qualified staff. Women found themselves in a majority among semi-qualified and unqualified staff and apprentices. Similarly, men constituted 73.9 per cent of holders of middle ranking diplomas, 72 per cent of holders of the *baccalauréat* and 63.8 per cent of holders of a degree. These statistics will doubtless change in a few years, given the increasing number of women who are currently registering in universities and institutes of higher education.

4.2.2.3 Authenticity

Portuguese law contains no information on this subject.

4.2.2.4 Security

The area of public security falls outside the principle of equal treatment. Women only have limited access to military careers.[2]

4.2.2.5 Religion

The clergy and members of religious orders fall outside the principle of equal treatment.

4.2.2.6 Decency and privacy

It is established that the post of physical education teacher is open to members of both sexes. In hospitals, equal access to all positions is a right.

---

1 See §3.8.2.3 above and §4.8.2 below.

2 See §4.2.1.4 above.

4.2.2.7 Single-sex establishments

Portuguese law contains no information on this subject.

4.3 TERRITORIAL SCOPE

The principle of equality applies to the whole of the territory of Portugal, including the islands of the Azores and Madeira.

4.4 PERSONAL SCOPE

4.4.1 EMPLOYEES

All workers with a contract of employment are covered by the equal treatment principle.[1]

4.4.2 INDEPENDENT CONTRACTORS

Self-employed persons do not come within the field of application of Decree (DL) No 392/79 of 20 September 1979, as they are not bound by a contract of employment.

4.4.3 HOME WORKERS

See Chapter 3 above.[2]

4.4.4 PUBLIC SECTOR

Decree (DL) No 426/88 of 18 November 1988 extended the principles established by Decree (DL) No 392/79 of 20 September 1979 to workers employed in public administration.

4.4.5 DOMESTIC EMPLOYEES

As stated previously, this category is covered by employment law.[3] The principle of equal treatment covers these employees.

4.4.6 NON-EMPLOYED POPULATION

The non-employed population falls outside the principle of equal treatment.

---

1 Article 2(b) of Decree (DL) No 392/79 of 20 September 1979.
2 See §3.3.3 above.
3 See §3.3.5 above.

4.4.7 OTHER WORKERS

Article 20(1) of Decree (DL) No 392/79 of 20 September 1979 provided that the regulation of the status of persons employed in private houses would be fixed at a later date. Decree (DL) No 235/92 of 24 October 1992 took this up.

4.5 ACTIVITIES COVERED

All professional activities, in the public as well as in the private sector, are covered by the principle of equal treatment.

4.6 COMPARATOR

As in equal pay, the application of the principle of equal treatment can be reviewed in relation to the same employer and for a contemporaneous job. All other comparisons are made for statistical or study purposes only.

4.7 HIRING

4.7.1 RECRUITMENT METHODS

Recruitment in the private sector follows the law of the market and is carried out through advertisements of vacancies, interviews, tests etc. Decree (DL) No 392/79 of 20 September 1979 requires non-discriminatory treatment in this regard. It has however proved difficult to establish proof of infringement of this equality principle, except in cases of flagrant breach, as was encountered within the *Banco Comercial Português*.[1]

Recruitment to public office is conducted through advertisements of vacancies in the *Diário da República*. This competition may be followed by tests or interviews. Decree (DL) No 426/88 of 18 November 1988 requires the observance of the equality principle in these procedures. It should be noted that civil servants in the Army are subject to this system.

4.7.2 ADVERTISEMENTS

Job advertisements must not contain, directly or indirectly, any restriction, specification or preference based on sex.[2] Infringements of this rule may lead to an administrative fine (a *coima*),[3] imposed by the Department for the General Inspection of Work; sometimes it is necessary to bring a case before the Labour Tribunal (*Tribunal do Trabalho*) in order to ensure that this provision is respected.

1 See p. 17 above.

2 Article 7(1) of Decree (DL) No 392/79 of 20 September 1979.

3 Article 8 of Decree (DL) No 491/85 of 26 November 1985.

Article 7(2) of Decree (DL) No 392/79 of 20 September 1979 authorizes the imposition, at the time of recruitment, of physical requirements linked to the job or to the conditions in which it is exercised. It is possible, but only within these limits, to demand that workers are of a specified size.

4.7.3 JOB TITLE

The rules relating to job advertisements also apply to job titles.

4.7.4 JOB DESCRIPTION

The aforementioned rules apply to the job description. As has been noted, art. 7(2) of Decree (DL) No 392/79 of 20 September 1979 specifies that since recruitment may only be conducted on objective criteria, it is prohibited to formulate physical requirements which have no bearing on the job or the conditions in which it is exercised.

4.7.5 SELECTION ARRANGEMENTS

During hiring procedures it is forbidden to refer to, or to ask questions concerning such matters as the civil, family or pregnant state of the candidate.

4.7.6 TERMS ON WHICH A JOB IS OFFERED

Apart from the circumstances envisaged under the provisions of art. 7(2) of Decree (DL) No 392/79 of 20 September 1979, the employer must not take marital or family status or pregnancy into account. Infringements of this rule are very common in practice, but difficulties in establishing the relevant evidence usually prevents such violations from being brought before the courts.

4.7.7 REFUSAL OR DELIBERATE OMISSION TO OFFER A JOB

It is prohibited to refuse or deliberately to fail to offer a job for reasons related to sex. The freedom of action of the employer in the hiring process, however, renders proof of this almost impossible, unless the facts can be established clearly.[1]

4.8 WORKING CONDITIONS

4.8.1 RELATION TO PAY

Given the segmentation of the labour market in Portugal, it is not really possible to compare working conditions with remuneration. Nobody can

1 See the example of the *Banco Comercial Português,* cited at p. 17 above.

deny that the economic activities in which female workers are most heavily concentrated are also those which receive the lowest remuneration. The absence of objective criteria for evaluating the various tasks in all the sectors currently prevents us from reaching definite conclusions.

4.8.2 EDUCATION AND TRAINING

Equality in education is guaranteed under art. 74 of the Constitution.

Equality of opportunity and of treatment in relation to professional training is guaranteed under Decree (DL) No 392/79 of 20 September 1979.[1] It is incumbent on the State to promote and coordinate activities relating to careers guidance and professional training for women, as well as to take steps to reintegrate women who had previously left work (through measures such as re-training and professional guidance).[2]

Various problems stand in the way of an effective implementation of these standards. On one hand, stereotypes adopted by the whole population considerably hinder women's access to traditionally male areas of education. At secondary school level it is possible to observe that some options are taken up mostly by girls, and others are chosen mostly by boys. Differences in careers guidance are confirmed in higher education. Thus in 1989, while 54.4 per cent of university graduates were women, the strongest concentrations of women in universities were in the faculties of arts, teaching, education, sciences and mathematics. One might add that the careers guidance counsellors, who ought to be in a position to reduce students' apprehensions about deviating from familiar patterns, are themselves influenced by social attitudes relating to the division of the labour market: they try to ensure that they match the characteristics of the candidates to the various possibilities of training and of professions.

Moreover, women are not favoured by the policies of professional training within companies, and this prevents them from being promoted and from obtaining management positions. Of the participants in professional training carried out in 1989, only 13 per cent were women. Even in the sectors where women are predominant, women in professional training were less numerous than men. This is due primarily to the fact that training takes place outside of working hours, when women have to busy themselves with domestic and family-based tasks.

At State level, the Ministry of Employment and Social Security runs most professional training courses. The Institute for Employment and Professional Training, which was established in 1979, set up a network of persons responsible for equality of opportunity. A series of positive action

---

1 Article 6 of the Decree.

2 Article 5 of the Decree.

measures were taken, most especially in the form of financial incentives for companies hiring or training women in traditionally male areas. This Institute also drew up and carried out training programmes for young women in these areas and assisted their professional placement. The Commission for the Female Condition, in collaboration with other national organizations and with the support of the European Social Fund, also carried out several professional training projects (organization and management of small companies, use of new technology). Nevertheless, there are still obstacles to be overcome, especially concerning the development of professional technical teaching and the professional training of the long-term unemployed.

4.8.3 ACCESS TO BENEFITS, FACILITIES, SERVICES, PROMOTION

Article 58(3)(b) of the Constitution, as well as art. 10 of Decree (DL) No 392/79 of 20 September 1979, guarantee equality in relation to career development as a whole and in relation to access to management posts. However, these principles are not often reflected in practice, particularly because women are removed — often temporarily — from the labour market when they have children. Limitations resulting from the current organization of professional training also have a negative effect.[1]

4.9 EXCLUSION, DISMISSAL OR OTHER DETRIMENT

4.9.1 DISCIPLINARY SANCTIONS

A sanction is not permitted where it is taken against a worker who is exercising his rights,[2] especially that of claiming redress for discrimination based on sex.[3] In such cases, the worker will have the right to compensation.[4]

4.9.2 DISMISSAL

Dismissal without just cause is unlawful,[5] for example following a complaint alleging discrimination.[6] Article 11 of Decree (DL) No 392/79 of 20 September 1979 provides that in such cases the worker may demand compensation or any other remedy provided for by law. According to Decree (DL) No 64-A/89 of 27 February 1989, the employer is required to pay remuneration for the months between the date of dismissal and that of the

1 See §4.8.2 above.
2 Article 32(1)(d) of Decree (DL) No 49408 of 24 November 1969.
3 Article 11 of Decree (DL) No 392/79 of 20 September 1979.
4 Article 33 of Decree (DL) No 49408, and art. 11 of Decree (DL) No 392/79 of 20 September 1979.
5 Article 12(1)(c) of Decree (DL) No 64-A/89 of 27 February 1989, on the termination of the contract of employment; see also arts 9 and 12(5).
6 Article 11 of Decree (DL) No 392/79 of 20 September 1979.

judgment, as well as to ensure the reinstatement of the worker, unless the latter decides to opt for compensation.[1]

4.10 INSTRUCTIONS TO DISCRIMINATE

Portuguese law contains no particular information on this subject.

4.11 PRESSURE TO DISCRIMINATE

Portuguese law contains no particular information on this subject.

4.12 DISCRIMINATION BY AN EMPLOYEE OR A TRADE UNION

Sexual harassment constitutes a form of discrimination by a worker and may be challenged before the courts. However, there is not yet any legislation dealing specifically with sexual harassment in Portugal. In such cases, therefore, criminal law and employment law are applied.[2]

4.13 DISCRIMINATORY PRACTICES

Portuguese legislation relating to equal treatment is currently very comprehensive. Nevertheless, discriminatory practices are frequent: there is direct discrimination, tolerated or not suppressed due to lack of proof, for example in access to a post or to professional training; then, there is indirect discrimination which results from the division of the labour market.

Consequently, measures aiming to give equality of access remain necessary. Positive action measures may constitute an initial path to follow in order to achieve this. Employment legislation could also take account of benefits for supporting a family, so that they are granted to the husband and to the wife in the same manner. Other measures regarding family support should be taken,[3] particularly targeting the creation of infrastructures for childcare.[4]

Moreover, as the decision to employ women is taken in the final resort by the employer, the path of collective bargaining would seem to be more effective than legislation. Through this process, measures for homogenizing the labour market can more easily be taken, thanks to its greater clarity and to recourse to company reports.

---

1 Article 13 of the Decree.

2 See §2.2.2.4 above.

3 Article 22 of Law No 4/84 of 5 April 1984.

4 See the draft presented by the Social Democrat Party (PSD) of 10 March 1992.

4.14 SPECIAL TREATMENT

4.14.1 PROTECTIVE LEGISLATION

4.14.1.1 Pregnancy and maternity

The Constitution grants women the right to special protection during pregnancy and after childbirth, including adequate leave not involving any loss of remuneration or benefits.[1] The State is required to ensure working conditions which provide this protection.[2] Paternity and maternity are equally eligible for social protection.[3]

Law No 4/84 of 5 April 1984 regulates the protective framework for the public and private sectors: it governs maternity leave or paternity leave in the event of the death or incapacity of the mother, leave after adoption, absence from work for consultations or for breastfeeding, staying with sick children, the organization of working hours, prohibited work or work subject to restrictions, maternity and paternity subsidies in the event of sick minors. Decrees (DL) No 135/85 and No 136/85 of 3 May 1985 implement this Law for workers subject, respectively, to the legal context of the individual contract and to public administration. Ministerial Decree (P) No 186/73 of 13 March 1973 lists work prohibited for pregnant women.

Law No 4/84 of 5 April 1984 also provides that part-time work should be available to pregnant women.[4]

Despite this legislation, complaints linked to maternity sent to the Commission for Equality in Work and Employment are numerous, which leads to the conclusion that there are instances of discrimination in this area.

4.14.1.2 Parental leave and analogous measures

Staying with a child in hospital or with a sick child justifies, for a certain time, the absence of the parents from the workplace, without loss of rights.[5] The father or the mother may also interrupt their work for a period of six to 24 months.[6] Their reintegration at work is ensured.[7] Finally, workers with children who are less than 12 months old have the right to work for reduced or flexible hours.[8]

---

1 Article 60(3) of the Constitution.
2 Article 59(2)(c) of the Constitution.
3 Article 60(1) of the Constitution.
4 Article 15 of the Law; see also art. 17 of Decree (DL) No 136/85 of 3 May 1985.
5 Law No 4/84 of 5 April 1984.
6 Article 14 of Law No 4/84.
7 Article 15 of Decree (DL) No 136/85 and art. 16 of Decree (DL) No 135/85.
8 Article 15 of Law No 4/84.

4.14.1.3 Difficult or unpleasant working conditions

Women's working conditions are no harder than those of men. However, a woman's responsibility for household tasks and the care of the family affects her resistance. Moreover, it would appear that approximately one-third of women who work are victims of sexual harassment, with effects on their conditions of work. Studies show that the most frequent reaction to this is silence, due to ignorance of opportunities for redress.

Night work is no longer prohibited for women.[1] Furthermore, existing legislation does not restrict women's work where there are difficult working conditions.

4.14.2 POSITIVE ACTION

4.14.2.1 Definition

Positive action consists of programmes of action which are intended to increase the presence of women or other marginalized workers at all levels of the occupational hierarchy. Such action has as its object the correction of a factual situation through the adoption of transitory measures which establish a preference.

In Portuguese law, positive action is envisaged in Decrees (DL) No 392/79 of 20 September 1979 and No 426/88 of 18 November 1988.

Positive action should not be confused with the various legislative and administrative measures on equality, particularly those dealing with publicity, paternity and maternity, or education and family planning. Positive action has a wider scope and can be conducted both by the State and by private sector bodies.

4.14.2.2 Field of application

Article 59(3) of the Constitution gives the State the responsibility of ensuring equal opportunities in the choice of a profession or of a type of work and of eliminating obstacles to access to any post, employment or professional category. This is to be achieved through legislative measures intended to prevent discrimination in the field of work, but also through careers guidance and professional training which allow women to take up new professions and higher posts, to achieve re-training and re-integration etc. The higher level of female unemployment, which is in particular due to the crisis affecting certain sectors and certain professions, reinforces this need.

---

1 See §3.7.3 above.

Article 5 of Decree (DL) No 392/79 of 20 September 1979 echoes this constitutional provision. It also goes further in relation to careers guidance and training: in effect, it creates a framework of preference for single women with children and those aged between 14 and 19 or between 20 and 24 who do not have any qualifications or have not completed obligatory schooling. Moreover, the Ministry of Employment is responsible for fixing annually the percentage of women for whom access to professional training is guaranteed.

Article 3(2) of Decree (DL) No 392/79 and art. 9(2) of Decree (DL) No 426/88 provide for the legality of positive action.

4.14.2.3 Means

The correction of inequalities has been encouraged by trade unions for the private sector, and by the Secretariat for the Administration of Modernization for the Public Sector (*Secretariado de Modernização Administrativa para o Sector Público*). This encouragement has been accompanied by a series of recommendations to all departments on recruitment, training, promotion, conditions of employment etc. The aforementioned Secretariat especially wanted to promote the participation of women in management positions in public administration.

After Portugal joined the European Community and was granted access to the European Social Fund, it was hoped that certain training opportunities would be created. These opportunities were to be aimed primarily at young women in traditionally male professions.

In relation to professional training, most opportunities are initiated by the Ministry of Employment and Social Security. The Institute of Employment and Professional Training has adopted a whole series of positive action measures. These have most notably taken the form of financial incentives to companies which take on or train women in traditionally male jobs. Training projects in so called 'male' sectors have also been drawn up and implemented.[1]

4.14.2.4. Constitutional or legal problems

The adoption of positive action does not pose any constitutional or legal problems.[2] On the contrary, it contributes to the achievement of real equality as prescribed by art. 9 of the Constitution.[3] Moreover, developments at the international level are moving in this direction.[4]

---

1 See §4.8.2 above.

2 See §4.14.2.1 above.

3 See §2.1 above.

4 See in particular art. 4 of the Convention on the Elimination of all Forms of Discrimination Against Women of 18 December 1979.

It is, however, necessary to stress that special schemes aimed at women workers which have no foundation either in maternity protection or in the concept of positive action are unlawful.

5. SOCIAL SECURITY

5.1 DEFINITION OF SOCIAL SECURITY

5.1.1 STATUTORY SOCIAL SECURITY

Statutory systems include contributory and non-contributory schemes. They are governed by Law No 28/84 of 14 August 1984.

The contributory system includes, on one hand, the general system, which covers paid and self-employed workers, and on the other hand, special schemes. Membership of the general system is, in principle, obligatory for paid and self-employed workers: however, certain persons do not have to join, but may register voluntarily in accordance with terms fixed by the law. Special systems are obligatory or optional. They cover either specific groups (such as railway employees and agricultural workers still under the old system) or other groups of workers (such as, employees in private homes and agricultural workers). Voluntary social insurance, the pecuniary payments of which are nevertheless more restricted, constitutes an optional system, to which housewives in particular may subscribe.

The contributory system covers instances of temporary incapacity and invalidity, sickness, maternity, workplace accidents and professional illnesses, death, old age, unemployment, the family. Health cover is ensured by the national health service. Incapacity due to an occupational accident will be covered by contractual insurance.

The non-contributory system aims to protect, in situations of economic or social failure, persons who are not covered by the contributory system. This protection is ensured via cash payments or benefits in kind to assist in family responsibilities, invalidity, old age, and the death of a close relative.

Social protection in the public service is the responsibility of the Ministry of Finances and is organized completely autonomously.

5.1.2 OCCUPATIONAL SOCIAL SECURITY

In Portugal there are complementary or contractual professional social security systems, made available by undertakings to their workers.

5.1.3 SOCIAL ASSISTANCE

Social security institutions may supply 'personalized' social action services with the aim, on one hand, of preventing hardship, failure and social marginalization, and, on the other hand, of social integration.

Social assistance is granted on a case-by-case basis: in contrast with the non-contributory system, it does constitute a right, but is granted according to need.

5.2 SOCIAL SECURITY DIRECTIVES AND OTHER LEGISLATION

5.2.1 ARTICLE 119 OF THE EEC TREATY

The ECJ has declared that working conditions, such as the consequences of provisions recommending a different retirement age, do not fall within the field of application of art. 119 of the EEC Treaty.[1] The retirement age, which in the private sector in Portugal is 65 years for men and 62 years for women, is therefore not covered by this article.

Moreover, statutory social security payments, especially retirement pensions, do not constitute indirectly paid benefits within the sense of art. 119(2).[2]

As for complementary benefits, Decree (DRegul.) No 12/83 of 12 February 1983 on the basis of calculation for social security contributions excludes further subsidies for sickness and pensions, which are thus not considered as remuneration in social security law.

On the other hand, contributions paid by the employer to a retirement scheme by means of a complementary amount of gross pay constitute remuneration within the terms of art. 119(2) of the EEC Treaty. There is therefore discrimination where these are paid only to male workers.[3]

5.2.2 DIRECTIVE 75/117/EEC

See §5.2.1 above.

5.2.3 DIRECTIVE 76/207/EEC

General policies for termination of contracts at retirement age — which is different for men and for women — fall within the field of application of

---

1 *Defrenne* v. *Sabena*, Case 149/77, [1978] ECR 1365 (ECJ).

2 *Defrenne* v. *Belgian State*, Case 80/70, [1971] ECR 445 (ECJ).

3 *Worringham* v. *Lloyds Bank Ltd*, Case 69/80, [1981] ECR 767 (ECJ).

Directive 76/207/EEC and are thus discriminatory.[1] According to information which we have gathered, such general dismissal policies do not exist in Portugal.

5.2.4 DIRECTIVE 79/7/EEC

The fixing of a different retirement age for the granting of social security payments, especially pensions, does not constitute a breach of Directive 79/7/EEC.[2]

All discrimination in social security matters in Portugal has been eliminated or will be in the near future.

5.2.5 DIRECTIVE 86/613/EEC

Wives of self-employed or agricultural workers have access to the contributory social security system. In the case of maternity, the various payments are also attributed, except the subsidy for staying with sick children.

However, partners of agricultural workers may not register, as the low level of revenues from small scale agricultural holdings does not permit the payment of social security contributions by both partners; it is very often the woman who does not register.

5.3 PROBLEMATIC CONCEPTS

5.3.1 BREADWINNER

This concept does not exist in Portuguese law.

5.3.2 SOLE BREADWINNER

This concept does not exist in Portuguese law.

5.3.3 HEAD OF HOUSEHOLD

This notion has been removed from Portuguese law.

---

1 *Marshall* v. *Southampton and South-West Hampshire Area Health Authority*, Case 152/84, [1986] ECR 723 (ECJ).

2 Article 7(1)(a) of the Directive.

5.3.4 COHABITANT

Certain recent laws have treated unions between cohabitants in a similar way to that applying to marriage, for example in the context of survivors' pensions (in the public and private sector) and certain subsidies. For instance, some pensions (*pensão social*) are granted only to those who have no resources and who do not benefit from social security. This right depends on the resources of the whole family, to which the cohabitant belongs. Moreover, the concept of 'partner' is likely to be widely interpreted.

5.3.5 LIVING ALONE

This concept does not exist in Portuguese law.

5.3.6 DEPENDANT

In social security law, there is no general definition of the notion of a 'dependant'. Nevertheless, this concept is used in various contexts, such as unemployment[1] and family allowances.

5.4 EXCEPTIONS

5.4.1 RETIREMENT AGE

In the private sector, the retirement age is 65 years for men and 62 for women,[2] except for certain professions which are considered to be tiring, such as those of miner or sailor.[3] Furthermore, the age is 60 years for men and women who are not entitled to unemployment assistance.[4]

The age for access to old-age pensions, paid within the scope of the non-contributory system, is 65 years for both sexes.

The retirement age in the public service is the same for men and for women: 60 years of age and 36 years of service; retirement is obligatory at the age of 70.[5]

5.4.2 SEX AS A DETERMINING FACTOR

In so far as the labour market is divided in such a way that women earn less than men, they will pay lower contributions and will also receive lower

1 See art. 16 of Decree (DL) No 79-A/89 of 13 March 1989.

2 Article 88(2) of Decree (DRegul.) No 45266 of 23 September 1963.

3 Article 88(3) of Decree (DRegul.) No 45266 of 23 September 1963; here the age is reduced.

4 Article 36 of Decree (DL) No 79-A/89 of 13 March 1989.

5 Articles 35 to 38 of Decree (DL) No 498/72 of 9 December 1972.

pensions. Moreover, many women interrupt their work for a certain time in order to care for their families. This factor also works against them, given that social security payments depend on the duration of periods of work.

As for maternity, women are often beneficiaries of cash payments. Under certain conditions, fathers may also claim them.

5.5 LEVELLING UP/DOWN

Eligibility for social security payments depends on the payment of contributions which, themselves, are a percentage of remuneration. At the present time, in view of the fact that Decree (DL) No 392/79 of 20 September 1979 equalized remuneration upwards in the event of discrimination, social security payments will follow the same trend.

5.6 PART-TIME WORK

In principle, part-time workers have the right to all social security payments, the amount being in proportion to their work.

Women are the main participators of this system; they are also subject to the consequences at social security level.

6. ENFORCEMENT OF THE PRINCIPLE

6.1 COURT OR TRIBUNAL PROCEDURE

6.1.1 ACQUIRING THE EVIDENCE

6.1.1.1 Prescribed forms

In employment law in Portugal, the rules of evidence are flexible: all kinds of evidence are admissible. The admissibility and value of various kinds of evidence are provided for by law. Facts may especially be proved by presumptions, witness accounts, written reports and expertise.

In order to influence the judge's personal conviction, the parties may use any matter likely to demonstrate the facts.

6.1.1.2 Obligation to furnish all relevant evidence

Portuguese legislation is strongly influenced by the principle of inquiry, while respecting the evidence of witnesses concerning the allegations of fact. The judge may proceed with any steps necessary in order to discover the truth of any facts alleged by the parties. The judge takes account of all proof submitted, whether or not it originates from the party with the burden of proof. It is the truth which matters and it is incumbent on each party to supply the evidence of what they are alleging. Moreover, the Code of Labour Procedure[1] imposes on the parties the necessity of collaborating in the trial by disclosing and supplying clarifications at any stage of the process, every time the law so requires or the judge deems it necessary.[2]

6.1.1.3 Annual information to works councils

The conditions for publication (and thus for the coming into force) of collective agreements do not include provisions relating to equality.[3] Communication to trade unions of information concerning the equality principle is therefore not obligatory.

6.1.2 BURDEN OF PROOF

In the private sector, the burden of proof rests with the employer in the proceedings relating to equal pay, and with the male or female worker in

---

1 Decree (DL) No 272-A/81 of 30 September 1981.

2 Article 28 of the Decree.

3 Articles 23 and 24 of Decree (DL) No 519-C1/79 of 29 December 1979.

matters of equal treatment.[1] A reversal of the burden of proof would however also be justified in the case of equal treatment. In fact, the injured party often encounters problems in establishing the evidence and problems caused by social prejudices which invariably affect the judiciary, which is still mainly composed of men.

On the other hand, in the public sector there is always a reversal of the burden of proof.[2]

6.1.3 COSTS

According to the general law, which also applies to the area of work, it is incumbent on the party who loses a case to bear its costs.

6.1.4 LEGAL AID

Legal aid is granted to persons who do not have the financial means to bear the costs incurred in the trial. It may cover the costs of the lawyer, as well as cover advance payments of expenses. Consequently, this protection is available to women who are experiencing financial difficulties.

Moreover, the Public Ministry may represent workers, and this ought in theory to facilitate women's access to justice.[3]

6.1.5 REMEDIES

6.1.5.1 Nullity/annulment

Any provisions contrary to equality are invalid. A worker or his or her trade union may bring an action relating to a contract of employment before the labour tribunal.[4]

Trade unions and employers' associations, as well as workers and employers, may ask the labour tribunal to declare a collective agreement to be invalid.[5] Administrative provisions may be the subject of an action before the administrative tribunals. It is possible for legislative provisions to be annulled by the Constitutional Tribunal.

---

1 Article 9(4) of Decree (DL) No 392/79 of 20 September 1979.

2 Article 10 of Decree (DL) No 426/88 of 18 November 1988.

3 Article 8 of the Constitution.

4 Article 64 of Law No 38/87 of 23 December 1987, and art. 16 of Decree (DL) No 392/79 of 20 September 1979.

5 Article 43 of Decree (DL) No 519-C1/79 of 29 December 1979.

6.1.5.2 Termination of discriminatory conduct

In the event of a finding of unlawful conduct, the employer is compelled to terminate the discriminatory act. A wrongful dismissal[1] may lead to the reinstatement of the worker.[2]

In the event of a sentence being passed in a criminal case, it is not possible to defer the penalty by ordering that certain measures should be taken. Fines do not exist in Portuguese law.

6.1.5.3 Declaration

Portuguese law contains no information on this subject.

6.1.5.4 Compensation

Unlawful measures taken by an employer will lead to a claim for compensation.[3] The worker who has been dismissed without just cause may opt for damages.

6.1.5.5 Recommendation

Portuguese law contains no information on this subject.

6.1.5.6 Positive enforceable order

There have never been any orders to take positive action in Portugal.

6.1.5.7 Positive action plan

Orders to initiate such programmes do not exist in Portugal.

6.1.5.8 Criminal and administrative sanctions

In the context of equality, the only infringements which may give rise to a criminal sentence are those resulting from sexual harassment.

Fines imposed by the Labour Inspectorate constitute administrative labour sanctions.[4]

---

1 See §4.9 above.

2 Article 11(3) of Decree (DL) No 392/79 of 20 September 1979, and art. 13 of Decree (DL) No 64-A/89 of 27 February 1989.

3 Article 33 of Decree (DL) No 49408 of 24 November 1969, and art. 11 of Decree (DL) No 392/79 of 20 September 1979.

4 See art. 8 of Decree (DL) No 491/85 of 26 November 1985.

6.1.6 CLASS ACTIONS

Class actions are not available in this field. Article 16(2) of Decree (DL) No 392/79 of 20 September 1979 and art. 11(3) of Decree (DL) No 426/88 of 18 November 1988, however, provide that an injured worker may ask his or her trade union to act on his or her behalf. Knowing that women workers may fear reprisals from their employer, the legislature introduced this measure with the aim of facilitating the application of the law.

6.1.7 EXCLUSION OF JUDICIAL REDRESS

In principle, any person who considers that they have been injured by discrimination based on sex has a right of access to justice.[1] Nevertheless, in practice the exercise of the right to redress is impeded by matters such as problems of proof (which may equally lead to considerable expenses), by the fear of reprisals on the part of the employer, by socio-cultural prejudice influencing judges.

6.1.8 TIME LIMITS

There is no time limit for the commencement of an action relating to provisions of collective agreements (before labour tribunals) or legislation (before the Constitutional Tribunal). Before labour tribunals, the time limit for actions relating to contracts of employment is one year, commencing on the date of the cessation of the contract. For actions to reject the modification of clauses in individual contracts of employment by company rules, the time allowed is one month commencing on the date of the execution of the contract or publication of the rule. Actions relating to administrative acts cannot be brought later than 60 days after the act or knowledge of it (before administrative tribunals). Criminal actions relating to infringements originating from the competence of labour tribunals cannot be brought later than two years after the date of the infringement.

6.2 COURTS AND TRIBUNALS

6.2.1 SPECIALIZED JURISDICTION

In Portugal, there is no specialized jurisdiction pertaining to equality.

The labour inspectorate draws up reports and imposes administrative sanctions. Appeals against these decisions are brought before labour

---

1 Article 16 of Decree (DL) No 392/79 of 20 September 1979.

tribunals. The latter consist either of a single judge,[1] or a college[2] to which, in certain cases, two social judges are attached.

6.2.1.1 Equality officer

This notion does not exist as such in Portuguese law. The latter only recognizes the labour inspectorate. It is incumbent on labour inspectors to review the application of employment laws. To this end, they sometimes request an opinion from the Commission for Equality at Work and in Employment. They also draw up reports and apply certain pecuniary sanctions whilst exercising their duties, but they lack any legal competence.

6.2.1.2 Arbitration court

There is no court of arbitration in this field.

6.2.1.3 Equal opportunities agency

No entity responsible for problems linked to equality is endowed with legal competence.

6.2.1.4 Conciliation procedures

In principle, conciliation procedures are supposed to take place prior to a hearing. The latter only occurs in the event of failure of conciliation.[3]

6.2.2 SPECIALIZED TRAINING FOR JUDGES

Specific training for judges in the field of equality does not exist, and to date there has not been a special refresher course to this end in Portugal. However, Portuguese judges receive training on the entire body of employment law at the Centre for Legal Studies.

6.2.3 SPECIALIZATION WITHIN THE SYSTEM

In Portugal, there is no specialization within the system.

---

1 Article 83 of Decree (DL) No 38/87 of 23 December 1987, containing the organic law governing judicial tribunals.

2 Article 79 of the same Decree.

3 Decree (DL) No 272-A/81 of 30 September 1981, containing the Code of Labour Procedure.

6.3 ENFORCEMENT AGENCY

6.3.1 TYPE

6.3.1.1 Labour inspectorate

As we have already seen,[1] there is a labour inspectorate in Portugal. It is an administrative authority, governed by Decree (DL) No 327/83 of 8 July 1983. Its responsibility is to carry out inspections in the context of the rules on equality.[2] It is incumbent on this body to ensure respect, on the one hand, for the standards of employment law contained in the laws, provisions of collective agreements and contracts of employment, and those relating to conditions of employment, and, on the other hand, for the standards relating to employment, protection in the event of unemployment and professional training.[3]

6.3.1.2 Equal opportunities agency

The Commission for Equal Opportunities at Work and in Employment (CITE), as well as the Commission for Equality and for the Rights of Women (CIDM), are subordinate to the Ministry of Employment and Social Security.

6.3.2 FUNCTIONS

6.3.2.1 Advice

The labour inspectorate is responsible for educating and guiding managers, employers and workers, by means of the provision of information and technical advice, with a view to securing an understanding of and respect for the laws, especially those which have a bearing on the equality principle.[4]

The CITE issues notices of advice to the Labour Inspectorate, judges, trade unions and employers' associations, to the body responsible for proceeding with conciliation in the event of individual conflicts at work or to any other interested party. It also considers complaints submitted to it by injured workers. Furthermore, it recommends the adoption of measures for the effective implementation of the rules on equality[5] to the Ministry of Employment and Social Security.

---

1 See §§6.2.1 and 6.2.1.1 above.
2 Article 17 of Decree (DL) No 392/79 of 20 September 1979.
3 Article 3(1)(a) and (b) of Decree (DL) No 327/83 of 8 July 1983.
4 Articles 3(1)(h) and 28 of Decree (DL) No 327/83 of 8 July 1983.
5 Article 15 of Decree (DL) No 392/79 of 20 September 1979.

The CIDM contributes to necessary legislative amendments, by proposing measures, by giving advice on drafts or proposals for laws and by initiating the creation of mechanisms necessary for effective respect for laws. It takes a position on questions relating to the status of women.[1] It also gives free legal advice.

6.3.2.2 Research

The CITE promotes the carrying out of studies and research, in order to eliminate discrimination against women at work.[2]

The CIDM carries out and supports inter-disciplinary research on the status of women. It insists especially that competent bodies are aware of the necessity to consider the statistics relating to the status of women.[3]

6.3.2.3 Legal aid

None of the afore-mentioned bodies gives legal aid, which is available as of right in instances of insufficient financial means.[4]

6.3.3 REMEDIES

6.3.3.1 Notice

The labour inspector draws up a report when he finds, in person and directly, any infringement of the standards which are subject to his control.[5]

6.3.3.2 Injunction

No body issues an injunction in the event of an infringement of the rules relating to equality. The labour inspectorate may, however, suspend the application of an administrative sanction for a certain time, during which compensation for the infringement may be paid or the situation rectified.

Moreover, it is obligatory for the advice which the CITE sends to the Labour Inspectorate to be followed once it has been officially approved by the Minister.

---

1 Article 3(1) of Decree (DL) No 166/91 of 9 May 1991.

2 Article 15(1)(b) of Decree (DL) No 392/79 of 20 September 1979.

3 Articles 2(1)(a) and 3(1)(e) of Decree (DL) No 166/91 of 9 May 1991.

4 See however §6.1.4 above.

5 Articles 29 and 32 *et seq.* of Decree (DL) No 327/83 of 8 July 1983, and arts 48 to 50 of Decree (DL) No 491/85 of 26 November 1985.

6.3.3.3 Compensation

Damages may only be granted by a judge.

6.4 COLLECTIVE AGREEMENTS

The instruments of collective labour regulation (IRCT: *instrumentos de regulamentação colectiva do trabalho*) constitute the whole of the collectively agreed, arbitration or administrative standards applicable to professional relationships set up between the parties.

A collective agreement (*acordo*) is agreed between several employers and one or more trade unions. A collective contract is agreed between one or more employers' associations and one or more trade unions. A company agreement is agreed between one employer and one or more trade unions. It is possible to adhere to a collective agreement (*convenção*) by means of an 'adherence agreement' (*acordo*). A Ministerial extension decree extends an IRCT to employers and workers who were not included amongst the parties. A Ministerial labour decree is issued where recourse to another type of IRCT proves impossible. The two latter types of IRCT originate jointly from the Minister for Employment and Social Security and from the Minister responsible for the sector concerned. Finally, the parties may (or must, in certain instances) submit to a commission composed of three arbitrators the conflicts which occurred at the time of the conclusion or revision of a collective agreement (*convenção*). The arbitration decision has the same effect as the collective agreement.

The question here is what happens to such collective agreements where they contain discriminatory clauses affecting workers of a specific sex. The response is given in arts 12 and 13 of Decree (DL) No 392/79 of 20 September 1979. The discriminatory provisions will be invalid and without effect.

6.4.1 EQUAL PAY CLAUSE

Article 22(4) of Decree (DL) No 392/79 of 20 September 1979 states that collective agreements must contain, wherever possible, provisions implementing the rules on equality.

6.4.2 AUTOMATIC NULLITY

See §6.1.5.1 above.

6.4.3 COLLECTIVE REDRESS

Article 16(2) of Decree (DL) No 392/79 of 20 September 1979 provides that the injured worker may ask his or her trade union to act on his or her behalf.

Article 6 of Decree (DL) No 272-A/81 of 30 September 1981 admits trade unions and employers' associations as legitimate parties in actions relating to collective interests which they are legally required to attend.

Article 43 of Decree (DL) No 519-C1/79 of 29 December 1979 grants a power to review the legality of an IRCT to trade unions and employers' associations.

6.4.4 AGENCY MONITORING

The labour inspectorate is responsible for ensuring the application of the rules contained in an IRCT.[1]

The CITE recommends to the Minister the adoption of measures for the implementation of the equality principle. This task is aimed at commissions whose responsibility it is to prepare Ministerial labour decrees on employment. It also assists bodies who draft an IRCT, with the aim of establishing correct correlations between the professional categories and the corresponding remuneration.[2]

---

1 Article 3 of Decree (DL) No 327/83 of 8 July 1983.

2 Article 15 of Decree (DL) No 392/79 of 20 September 1979.

SOURCES OF EQUALITY LAW

7. LEGISLATION

7.1 CONSTITUTIONAL PROVISIONS

7.1.1 CONSTITUTION OF 2 APRIL 1976[1]

Article 13 – Principle of equality

1. All citizens shall have the same social status and shall be equal before the law.

2. No person shall be privileged, favoured, disadvantaged, deprived of any right or freed from any duty because of his ancestry, sex, race, language, country of origin, religion, political or ideological convictions, education, economic situation or social condition.

Article 47 – Freedom of choice of profession and access to public office

1. All persons shall have the right freely to choose their profession or type of work, except where there are legal restrictions based on the collective interest or for reasons relating to ability.

2. All citizens shall have the right of access to public office, under the conditions of equality and liberty, in principle through competition.

...

Article 48 – Participation in public life

1. All citizens shall have the right to make representations or complaints in defence of their rights, of the Constitution, of laws or in the general interest, individually or collectively, to the organs of sovereignty or to any other authority.

...

Article 53 – Security in employment

Security in employment shall be guaranteed to workers, and dismissals without just cause or for political or ideological reasons shall be prohibited.

Article 58 – Rights at work

1. All persons shall have the right to work.

---

1 Current version, with full account taken of the amendments of 8 July 1989.

2. The duty to work is inseparable from the right to work, except for those who suffer from diminished ability for reasons of age, sickness or invalidity.

3. It shall be incumbent on the State, through the implementation of economic and social policy plans, to guarantee the right to work by ensuring:

(a) the implementation of full employment policies;
(b) equality of opportunity in the choice of profession or type of work, as well as the conditions of work, in order that access to any office, work or professional category is not closed or limited on the basis of sex;
(c) the cultural, technical and professional training of workers.

Article 59 – Workers' rights

1. All workers, without distinction as to age, sex, race, citizenship, country of origin, religion, political or ideological convictions, shall have the right to:

(a) remuneration for work, in accordance with its quantity, nature and quality, applying the principle of 'equal pay for equal work', in such a way as to guarantee a minimum standard of living;
(b) the organization of work in socially acceptable conditions, in such a way as to allow personal fulfilment;
(c) carry out their work in hygienic and safe conditions;
(d) rest and leisure, up to a maximum period of the length of the working day, to weekly rest times and to periodic paid holidays;
(e) to material assistance, where they find themselves involuntarily in a state of unemployment.

2. It is incumbent on the State to ensure working conditions, remuneration and rest periods to which workers have a right, especially:

...

(c) special protection of women's work during pregnancy and after childbirth.

...

Article 63 – Social security

1. All persons shall have the right to social security.

...

Article 68 – Paternity and maternity

1. Fathers and mothers shall have the right to the protection of society and of the State in the fulfilment of their irreplaceable role in caring for children, especially regarding education, without detriment to their professional fulfilment and to their participation in the civic life of the country.

2. Maternity and paternity constitute important social values.

3. Women workers shall have the right to special protection during pregnancy and after childbirth, including leave for an adequate period, without loss of remuneration or benefits.

Article 74 – Education

1. All persons shall have the right to education, and the right to equality of opportunity, access to schooling and scholastic success shall be guaranteed for all.

...

7.2 NATIONAL LAWS RATIFYING INTERNATIONAL TREATIES

1. Decree (DL) No 27891 of 26 July 1937, ratifying ILO Convention No 45 of 21 June 1935, concerning the employment of women underground in mines of all categories.[1]

2. Decree (DL) No 42520 of 23 September 1959, ratifying ILO Convention No 111 of 25 June 1958, prohibiting discrimination in access to professional training, access to employment and conditions of employment.[2]

3. Decree (DL) No 44862 of 23 September 1963, ratifying ILO Convention No 89 of 9 July 1948, concerning night-work for women employed in industry.[3]

4. Decree (DL) No 47302 of 4 November 1966, ratifying ILO Convention No 100 of 29 June 1951, concerning equal pay for male and female workers for work of equal value.[4]

5. Law No 29/78 of 12 June 1978, ratifying the International Covenant of the United Nations on Civil and Political Rights, signed in New York on 16 December 1966.[5]

6. Law No 45/78 of 11 July 1978, ratifying the International Covenant of the United Nations on Economic, Social and Cultural Rights, signed in New York on 16 December 1966.[6]

---

1 D.R., 1st series, 26 July 1937.
2 D.R., 1st series, 23 September 1959.
3 D.R., 1st series, 23 January 1963.
4 D.R., 1st series, 4 November 1966.
5 D.R., 1st series, 12 June 1978.
6 D.R., 1st series, 11 July 1978.

7. Law No 65/78 of 13 October 1978, ratifying the European Convention for the Protection of Human Rights and Fundamental Freedoms, signed in Rome on 4 November 1959.[1]

8. Law No 23/80 of 26 June 1980, ratifying the UN Convention on the Elimination of All Forms of Discrimination Against Women, signed in New York on 18 December 1979.[2]

9. Decree (DRegul.) No 112/80 of 23 October 1980, ratifying the UN Convention on the Elimination of Discrimination in Education, signed in Paris on 14 December 1960.[3]

10. Decree (DRegul.) No 63/84 of 10 October 1984, ratifying ILO Convention No 103 of 28 June 1952 concerning the protection of maternity.[4]

11. Decree (DRegul.) No 66/84 of 11 October 1984, ratifying ILO Convention No 156 of 23 June 1981 concerning equality of opportunity for workers of both sexes: workers having family responsibilities.[5]

12. Resolution No 22/85 of the Assembly of the Republic of 18 September 1985, ratifying the Treaty of Accession of the Kingdom of Spain and of the Republic of Portugal to the European Economic Community, signed in Madrid and Lisbon on 12 June 1985.[6]

13. Decree (DRegul.) No 38/91 of 6 August 1991, ratifying the European Social Charter of the Council of Europe, signed in Turin on 18 October 1961.[7]

7.3 NATIONAL TEXTS IMPLEMENTING EC DIRECTIVES

Decree (DL) No 392/79 of 20 September 1979 implements Directives 75/117/EEC and 76/207/EEC. Decree (DL) No 426/88 of 18 November 1988 extends the scope of Decree (DL) No 392/79, with a view to applying it to workers in public administration (as provided for in art. 20(2) of the latter). It also modifies several provisions relating to the Commission for Equality in Work and in Employment. In social security matters, Law No 28/84 of 14 August 1984 should be noted in the context of the implementation of the equality principle.

---

1 D.R., 1st series, 13 October 1978.
2 D.R., 1st series, 26 June1980.
3 D.R., 1st series, 23 October 1980.
4 D.R., 1st series, 10 October 1984.
5 D.R., 1st series 11 October 1984.
6 D.R., 1st series, 18 September 1985.
7 D.R., 1st series, 6 August 1991.

7.3.1 PROVISIONS RELEVANT TO EQUAL PAY AND EQUAL TREATMENT

7.3.1.1 Decree (DL) No 392/79 of 20 September 1979[1]

Article 1

1. The present law seeks to guarantee equality for women with men in relation to opportunities and treatment at work and in employment, arising out of the right to work provided for in the Constitution of the Republic of Portugal.
2. The provisions of the present law shall also be applied, together with any necessary adaptations, to potential discriminatory situations or practices against men.

Article 2

For the purposes of the present law, the following definitions apply:

(a) *discrimination*: any distinction, exclusion, restriction or preference based on sex, which has as its aim or result to compromise or refuse to recognize the enjoyment or the exercise of rights guaranteed by employment legislation;
(b) *employer*: any natural person or corporate body having the power to conclude, as employer, individual contracts of employment;
(c) *remuneration*: a payment of any kind from an employer to which a worker has a right under an individual contract of employment, whether or not it takes the form of remuneration, made in kind or in cash, especially: basic remuneration, ..., seniority payments, holiday and Christmas pay, productivity bonuses, commission on sales, general expenses, travel expenses, expenses for errors, remuneration for night-work, overtime, work during weekly rest days and work during public holidays, expenses for shifts, subsidies for meals rented accommodation, housing or merchandise;
(d) *equal work*: work carried out for the same employer, where the tasks accomplished are the same or of an objectively similar nature;
(e) *work of equal value*: work carried out for the same employer, where the tasks accomplished, although of a different nature, are considered as equivalent following the application of objective criteria of a job evaluation.

Article 3

1. The right to work implies the absence of any discrimination, direct or indirect, based on sex, especially by reference to civil or family status.

---

1 D.R., 1st series, 20 September 1979.

2. Provisions of a temporary nature which establish a preference based on sex shall not be considered as discriminatory where this is caused by the necessity to correct an unequal practice, as well as measures which tend to protect maternity as a social value.[1]

Article 11

1. All employers shall be prohibited from dismissing, applying sanctions or damaging a female worker in any form whatsoever, due to the submission by the latter of a complaint alleging discrimination.

2. Until evidence to the contrary is established, the application of any sanction to a female worker shall be presumed to be abusive, up to one year after the date of a complaint alleging discrimination.

3. A violation of the provision contained in para. 1 of the present article shall confer on a female worker the right to compensation in accordance with the general principles of law, which shall be added to any other damages provided for by law.

Article 14

1. The Commission for Equality in Work and Employment is established within the Ministry of Labour, with the aim of promoting the application of the provisions of the present law.

[[2]...]

---

1 Corrected in D.R., 1st series, 24 December 1979.

2 Repealed by Decree (DL) No 426/88 of 18 November 1988; D.R., 1st series, 18 November 1988.
Decree (DL) No 426/88 extended the competence of the Commission (art. 13) and modified its composition as follows (art. 14):

1. The Commission for Equality in Work and in Employment shall from now on be composed of:
   (a) two representatives from the Ministry of Employment and Social Security; one of whom shall preside;
   (b) one representative from the Ministry for Planning and Administration of the territory;
   (c) one representative of the member of the Government responsible for public functions;
   (d) one representative from the Commission for the Female Condition;
   (e) two representatives of union associations;
   (f) two representatives of employers' associations.
2. The Commission shall duly deliberate in the presence of the majority of its members and, in the event of a split, the president shall have the casting vote.
3. Administrative support shall be provided to the Commission by the Institute for Employment and Professional Training.
4. The cost of personnel and the operation of the Commission shall be supported out of the budget of the Institute of Employment and Professional Training.
5. The regulation of the operation of the Commission shall be approved by joint decision of the Minister for Employment and Social Security and by the member of the Government responsible for public functions.

Article 15

[1 1. It shall be incumbent on the Commission for Equality in Work and in Employment to:

(a) make recommendations to the Minister responsible for the sector of work, with a view to the adoption of legislative, regulatory and administrative measures aimed at perfecting the implementation of the standards contained in the present law;

(b) promote the carrying out of studies and investigations, with the aim of eliminating discrimination affecting women at work and in employment;

(c) stimulate and promote actions aiming to publicize the objectives of the present law;

(d) to make public, by any means available, obvious instances of violation of the standards of the present law, as long as the decision to make them known is taken unanimously by its members or with the agreement of the Minister responsible for the sector of work;

(e) promote the assistance of bodies responsible for drawing up instruments of collective labour regulation (*Instrumentos de regulamentação colectiva do trabalho*), with a view to setting up correct correlations between the various professional categories and the remuneration which corresponds to them;

(f) issue and approve advice concerning equality at work and in employment, each time they are requested to do so by the Work Inspectorate, by the judge of a case, by trade unions and employers' associations, by the body responsible for proceeding with an attempt to conciliate in individual work conflicts, or by any other interested party;

(g) ensure the carrying out of visits to work premises or request the Labour Inspectorate to do so, with the aim of revealing any discriminatory practices;

(h) maintain office support, direct the respective services and, in general, guarantee the conditions necessary for the development of its activity.

2. It shall be obligatory for the competence granted by sub-paragraph (a) of the preceding paragraph to be exercised with respect to the commissions responsible for drawing up ministerial decrees of labour regulation.

3. While exercising its competence, the Commission may ask for information and advice from any public or private body, as well as for the collaboration of any assessors which it may need.

4. In employment matters, the Commission shall co-ordinate its activities with the National Council of the Plan.]

---

1 Amended by Decree (DL) No 426/88 of 18 November 1988.

Article 16

1. Actions concerned with the implementation of the provisions of the present law may be brought before competent tribunals.

2. The right of action to which the preceding paragraph refers shall be exercised by a worker who considers that he has been discriminated against, or if he so desires, by a trade union representing him.

Article 17

...[1]

Article 23

1. All statutory, regulatory and administrative provisions contrary to the principle of free access for women to all employments, professions or positions of employment, including those which refer to criteria of selection, regardless of the sector or branch of activity, at all levels of the professional hierarchy, are repealed.

...

7.3.2 PROVISIONS RELEVANT TO EQUAL PAY

7.3.2.1 Decree (DL) No 392/79 of 20 September 1979[2]

Article 9

1. Equal remuneration between male and female workers for equal work or for work of equal value carried out for the same employer shall be guaranteed.

2. Variations in actual remuneration do not constitute discrimination where they are based on objective criteria of attribution, common to men and women.

3. A system of job descriptions and of job evaluation must be based on objective criteria common to men and to women, in such a way as to exclude any discrimination based on sex.

4. It is incumbent on a female worker who is alleging discrimination to show the basis of this allegation by referring to the worker(s) in comparison with whom she considers herself to have been discriminated; it is incumbent on the employer to prove that differences in actual remuneration are based on a factors other than sex.

---

1 This article grants competence to the Labour Inspectorate to control the implementation of the law and makes provision for sanctions.

2 D.R., 1st series, 20 September 1979.

Article 12

...

2. Provisions contained in instruments of collective labour regulation which establish, for the same professional categories or for equivalent professional categories, lower remuneration for women are also invalid and without effect, and they shall in law be replaced by the remuneration granted to men.

3. In the context of the provision in the preceding paragraph, the professional category shall be deemed to be the same or equivalent where a job evaluation finds it to amount to equal work or work of equal value respectively.

Article 13

1. The provisions of instruments of collective labour regulation which establish different remuneration for women apprentices, at the same stage of apprenticeship, measured on the basis of the passage of time, shall be invalid and shall have no effect.

2. In the instances listed in the last part of the preceding paragraph, the corresponding remuneration paid to male apprentices shall replace the one which was established by the invalid provision.

7.3.3 PROVISIONS RELEVANT TO EQUAL TREATMENT

7.3.3.1 Decree (DL) No 392/79 of 20 September 1979[1]

Article 4

1. Access for women to all employments, professions or positions of employment shall be guaranteed.

2. Save as what is provided in article 8, the following shall be considered as invalid and without effect: statutory and regulatory provisions, as well as the provisions of instruments of collective labour regulation, individual contracts of employment, company regulations, statutes of trade unions or independent professions and regulations governing access to a profession, which, in some way, limit the access of women to any employment, profession or position of employment.

Article 5

1. It shall be incumbent on the State to promote, encourage and co-ordinate activities concerned with professional guidance and training aimed at women, taking into account their motivation and employment patterns.

...

[1] D.R., 1st series, 20 September 1979.

4. The reintegration into employment of women who have interrupted their professional activity shall be the object of adequate measures, involving guidance as well as the availability of special refresher and proficiency courses.

Article 6

Employers shall ensure that women workers have equal opportunities and treatment with men in the context of professional training at all levels and of all kinds.

Article 7

1. Job advertisements and other forms of publicity linked to pre-selection and recruitment shall not contain, either directly or indirectly, any restriction or preference as to sex.
2. Recruitment for any position of employment shall be based exclusively on objective criteria, and the formulation of physical requirements which have no bearing on the professions or the conditions under which they are exercised shall be prohibited.
3. The following shall not constitute discrimination: recruitment limited to one sex or the other in activities linked with fashion, the arts or entertainment, when sex is essential to the nature of the task to be accomplished, rendering the task qualitatively different according to whether it is carried out by a man or a woman.

Article 8

1. Work which, according to the law, is considered to involve an actual or potential risk to the genetic system shall be prohibited or subjected to conditions.
2. Any statutory, regulatory or administrative provisions envisaged in the preceding paragraph shall be reviewed periodically on the basis of scientific and technical knowledge; in accordance with this knowledge, they shall be brought up-to-date, repealed or extended to all workers.

Article 10

1. The development of a professional career which gives access to the highest level in the hierarchy of a profession shall be guaranteed to women workers under the same conditions as those affecting men.
2. The right recognized in the preceding paragraph extends to management posts and to career changes.

Article 12

1. The following shall be invalid and without effect: provisions of instruments of collective labour regulation which establish professional categories intended specifically for male or female personnel; they are to be replaced by provisions covering both sexes.

...

4. Collective agreements shall include, wherever possible, provisions for the effective implementation of the provisions of the present law, especially through the participation of trade unions, in relation to selection and professional training.

7.3.3.2 Law No 4/84 of 5 April 1984 on the protection of maternity and paternity[1]

Chapter I – General principles

Article 1 – Paternity and maternity

1. Maternity and paternity constitute important social values.

2. Fathers and mothers shall have the right to protection by society and the State in carrying out their irreplaceable duties with respect to their children, especially regarding their education.

Article 2 – Equality of parents

1. Professional activity and participation in the civic life of the country shall be guaranteed to parents under conditions of equality.

...

4. Special rights in line with the biological cycle of maternity shall be guaranteed to mothers.

Article 3 – Duty to provide information concerning the system protecting maternity and paternity

1. It shall be incumbent on the State to provide information and to make known useful information relating to the rights of pregnant women, unborn children, children and parents, especially through social communication and the drawing up and free distribution of proper documentation.

...

---

1 D.R., 1st series, 5 April 1984.

Chapter III – Protection at work

Article 8 – Scope of application

The provisions of the present chapter shall apply to workers covered by the system of the individual contract of employment, including agricultural workers and employees in private houses, as well as workers in central, regional and local public administration, public institutes, administratively and financially autonomous public services and other bodies covered by public law, whatever their status.

Article 9 – Right of women to be excused from work

1. Women covered by the provisions of this chapter shall have the right to maternity leave of 90 days, 60 of which must be taken after the delivery, the other 30 days being taken, either wholly or partly, before or after delivery.
2. Exceptionally, following physical or psychological incapacity of the mother duly proved by a medical certificate, and for the duration of this condition, the last 30 or 60 days of maternity leave not immediately subsequent to the delivery may be taken by the father.
3. Where it is necessary to stay in hospital due to existing medical risks, the period of leave prior to the delivery may be increased by 30 extra days, without detriment to the right to 60 days after the delivery.
4. In the event of the mother or child having to stay in hospital during the period of leave after the delivery, this period may be interrupted, at the request of the mother, for the duration of the stay.
5. The period of leave following the delivery of a stillborn child or of a miscarriage shall be a minimum of 10 days and a maximum of 30 days, calculated on medical advice, duly justified, in line with the condition of the health of the mother.
6. If the new-born child dies within the period of leave following delivery, the latter shall terminate 10 days following the death, so long as the overall period following the delivery is not less than 30 days.

Article 10

1. If the mother dies during maternity leave following delivery, the father shall have the right to leave with a view to caring for his child; this leave shall be equal in length to that to which mother was still entitled and shall not be less than 10 days.
2. In the event of the death of a mother who does not work occurring during the 90 days following the delivery, the father of the new-born child shall have the right to leave equivalent to that described in the preceding paragraph, as adapted.

Article 11 – Adoption

...

A male or female worker who wishes to adopt a child shall have the right to be absent from work for 60 days in order to care for the child.

Article 12 – Dispensation for consultations and breast feeding

1. Pregnant women workers shall have the right to be excused from work with a view to being able to attend ante-natal consultations, for the duration and time as necessary and justified.

2. A mother who proves that she is breast-feeding her child shall have the right to be discharged from work, during each working day, for two separate periods of one hour at least, in order to be able to accomplish this; this right shall continue while she is still breast-feeding and until the child is one year old.

3. The right to be excused from work as contained in the present article shall not lead to any loss of remuneration or of any other benefit whatsoever.

Article 13 – Absence to care for sick children

1. Where there is an urgent and absolute need, workers have the right to be absent for up to 30 days per year in order to care for their biological or adopted children, or their step-children aged less than 10 years, in the event of illness or accident.

2. In the event of the child being admitted to hospital, the right to be absent extends to the period of duration of the hospital stay for a child aged less than 10 years; however, this right may not be exercised simultaneously by the father and the mother or by anyone who replaces them.

Article 14 – Special leave to care for children

1. A working father or mother shall have the right to interrupt their work for six months, commencing as from the end of maternity leave, in order to stay with the child; this term may be extended for a maximum of two years.

...

Article 15 – Part-time work and flexible working hours

Workers who have one or more children under 12 years of age shall have the right to work a reduced or flexible schedule, under conditions to be specified.

Article 16 – Prohibited work or work subject to conditions

The law shall define work prohibited or subjected to restrictions which involves actual or potential risks to the medical condition of men or women, in accordance with the state of scientific and technical knowledge.

Article 17 – Inadvisable tasks

1. During pregnancy and up to three months after delivery, a female worker shall have the right not to carry out medically inadvisable tasks, especially strenuous tasks or those which entail the handling of dangerous or toxic substances or involving exposure to environmental conditions which would endanger health; this right does not imply that the worker is entitled to refuse to carry out tasks other than those which she carries out habitually, if these tasks are not inadvisable.

2. During a proven period of breast feeding, and for the duration of one year, a female worker shall have the right not to carry out tasks which would expose her to the absorption of noxious substances which could be absorbed into her milk.

3. The relevant departments of the health service shall publish and submit for periodic revision the list of dangerous or toxic products, as well as the environmental conditions which are dangerous to health referred to in the preceding paragraph.

4. A pregnant woman worker is exempt from carrying out legal obligations and functional duties which involve a risk to the unborn child.

Article 18 – System of absences and dispensations

The absences referred to in arts 9, 10, 11 and 13 shall not lead to the loss of any right whatsoever; they shall be treated, for all purposes, as periods of actual work, except in the context of remuneration.

Chapter IV — Social security and social action schemes

Article 19 – Maternity or paternity allowance

During the periods of leave referred to in arts 9, 10 and 11, a male or female worker shall have the right to:

(a) an allowance equal to the average remuneration in question based on a calculation of the sickness allowance, where the party in question is covered by social security;

(b) the remuneration applicable to the public services, where the party in question is covered by the social protection system.

Article 20 – Allowance for caring for sick children

In the event of absences referred to in art. 13 and where there is no remuneration, the social security institutions shall grant a pecuniary allowance, the total amount of which shall not exceed the sickness allowance paid to a male or female worker, taking account of the conditions for recourse; this allowance will be increased progressively, within the limits of what is possible.

Article 21 – Extent of the access to social security payments

The periods of leave mentioned in art. 14 shall be taken into account for the calculation of payments from social protection systems in the event of invalidity or old age.

7.3.3.3 Decree (DL) No 135/85 of 3 May 1985[1]

This text contains the measures for implementation of Law No 4/84 of 5 April 1984 relating to the protection of maternity and paternity, affecting mothers and fathers working in central, regional and local administration, in public institutions, in autonomous public services and within other individual or public corporate bodies, whatever their status.

7.3.3.4 Decree (DL) No 136/85 of 3 May 1985[2]

This text contains the measures for implementation of Law No 4/84 of 5 April 1984, affecting working mothers and fathers covered by the legal system of the individual contract of employment, including agricultural workers and persons employed in private houses.

7.3.3.5 Decree (DL) No 154/88 of 29 April 1988[3]

This text expands Decree (DL) No 136/85 of 3 May 1985. It revises and improves the system in force, by means of the adoption of measures which allow for better satisfaction of the current needs of beneficiaries of social security schemes, where they are deprived of their remuneration following absences from work due to the birth of their children, the adoption of minors and care for sick dependants.

---

1 D.R., 1st series, 3 May 1985.

2 *Ibid.*

3 D.R., 1st series, 29 April 1988.

7.3.4 PROVISIONS RELEVANT TO EQUALITY IN SOCIAL SECURITY

7.3.4.1 Law No 28/84 of 14 August 1984 on social security[1]

Chapter I – Fundamental principles

Article 2 – Objectives of the system

1. The social security system shall protect workers and their families when they find themselves in situations of incapacity or reduced capacity to work and in involuntary unemployment. It shall also apply in the event of the death of a worker. It shall guarantee compensation for family responsibilities.
2. The social security system shall also protect persons who find themselves in a situation of reduced or inadequate means of subsistence.

Article 4 – Social security system

1. The social security system shall include social security schemes and institutions.
2. It is incumbent on social security institutions to manage social security schemes and to carry out social action intended to complete or replace the protection guarantee.

Article 5 – Principle of the social security system

1. The social security system shall apply the principles of universality, unity, effectiveness, decentralization, judicial guarantee, solidarity and participation.

...

4. Equality consists of the elimination of all discrimination, especially for reasons of sex or nationality, without detriment to the application of conditions of residence and reciprocity.

Chapter II — Social security and social action schemes
Section 2 — Social security schemes
Sub-section I — The general scheme

Article 18 – Scope of personal application

It shall be obligatory for salaried workers and self-employed workers to be included in the scope of application of the general scheme.

---

1 D.R., 1st series, 14 August 1984.

Article 19 – Scope of material application

1. The general scheme shall be applied by means of pecuniary or cash payments in the event of illness, maternity, occupational accidents and professional illnesses, unemployment, invalidity, old age, death, family responsibility, and other responsibilities provided for in the law.

2. Through necessary adaptations to be established by law, adoption shall have the same effect as birth for social security purposes.

Sub-section II — The non-contributory scheme

Article 28 – Objectives

The non-contributory scheme shall seek to achieve protection in situations of economic or social inadequacy not covered by the general scheme.

Article 29 – Scope of personal application

The non-contributory scheme shall cover national citizens and may be extended, in conditions established by law, to residents who are refugees, stateless and foreign persons.

Article 30 – Scope of material application

The non-contributory scheme shall be implemented by means of the granting of pecuniary payments or payments in kind, especially to compensate for family responsibilities and to ensure protection in the event of invalidity, old age and death.

Section 3 — Social action

Article 33 – Objectives

1. The fundamental aims of social action shall be the prevention of situations of inadequacy, dysfunction and social marginalization, and the achievement of community integration.

2. Social action shall also aim to ensure special protection for the most vulnerable groups, especially the young, the handicapped and the elderly, as well as other persons finding themselves in situations of economic or social inadequacy or under the effect of dysfunction or social marginalization, to the extent that these situations are not or cannot be resolved by social security schemes.

Article 35 – Guiding principles

Social action payments shall be paid according to priorities and to guidelines laid down by the Government; they shall aim in particular: ...

(d) to guarantee equality of treatment for potential beneficiaries.

7.4. OTHER NATIONAL TEXTS

7.4.1 DECREE (DL) NO 409/71 OF 27 SEPTEMBER 1971[1]

Article 31 – Night-work for women

1. Night-work for women in industrial establishments may only be authorized:
   (a) in the event of an Act of God which prevents normal functioning of workplaces;
   (b) where relevant materials are likely to change quickly and where night-work is considered indispensable to avoid their loss.
2. The conditions under which night-work for women may be authorized in the instances contained in sub-para. (b) of the preceding paragraph may be contained in collective agreements.
3. The instances of authorization mentioned in para. 1 are not applicable to women during pregnancy and until three months after delivery.

Article 32 – Women workers not protected by the prohibition of night-work

The following are not subject to the restrictions imposed by the preceding article:

(a) women who occupy posts of responsibility, of either a management or technical nature;

(b) women who are involved in services related to hygiene or well-being and who are not normally involved in manual work.

---

1 D.R., 1st series, 27 September 1971. The prohibition of night-work by women or its being subjected to certain conditions must be deemed to have been repealed by Decree (DL) No 392/79 of 20 September 1979 (arts 13 and 58(3)(b) of the Constitution and arts 3, 4, 8 and 23 of Decree (DL) No 392/79). See also *Criminal proceedings against Stoeckel*, Case C-345/89, 1991 [ECR] I-4047 (ECJ).

7.4.2 DECREE (DL) NO 251/74 OF 12 JUNE 1974,[1] DECREE (DL) NO 308/74 OF 6 JULY 1974,[2] AND DECREE (DL) NO 492/74 OF 27 SEPTEMBER 1974[3]

These texts open up access for women to careers in local administration, the diplomatic service and in the judiciary.

7.4.3 DECREE (DL) NO 166/91 OF 9 MAY 1991[4]

This text replaces the Commission for the Female Condition with the Commission for Equality and the Rights of Women.

Chapter I – Nature and attributions

Article 1 – Nature and objectives

1. The Commission for Equality and the Rights of Women, hereafter referred to as the 'Commission', shall be a body concerned with the study and analysis of the situation regarding equality of rights and opportunities, as well as with intervention in all areas which are related to the situation of women and equality. It shall pursue the following fundamental and permanent objectives:
   (a) to ensure that women and men enjoy the same opportunities, rights and dignities;
   (b) to achieve effective joint responsibility of women and men at all levels of family, professional, social, cultural, economic and political life;
   (c) to persuade society to recognize maternity and paternity as social functions and assumes the ensuing responsibilities.

...

3. The Commission shall replace, for all statutory purposes, the Commission for the Female Condition, which was established by Decree (DL) No 485/77 of 17 November 1977.

Article 3 – Tasks

1. The tasks of the Commission shall be as follows:
   (a) to intervene in the drawing up of overall and sectoral policy where it relates to the situation of women and equality of rights between women and men;
   (b) to contribute to legislative amendments deemed necessary in different areas, by proposing measures, by giving advice on drafts

---

1 D.R., 1st series, 12 June 1974.
2 D.R., 1st series, 6 July 1974.
3 D.R., 1st series, 27 September 1974.
4 D.R., 1st series, 9 May 1991.

or proposals for laws, and by initiating the creation of mechanisms which prove to be necessary for effective respect for laws;

(c) to promote activities which will lead to greater participation of women in development and in political and social life;

(d) to promote activities which will lead women and society as a whole to become aware of discrimination which women still suffer, in order to encourage them to act directly to advance their status and to guarantee that society accepts responsibility for the same objective;

(e) to undertake and encourage inter-disciplinary research on questions relating to equality and to the situation of women, especially in heightening the awareness of competent bodies of the necessity of statistical analysis of the situation of women in the areas in which they are involved, and to facilitate the dissemination of this research by means of seminars, symposiums, and other training activities;

(f) to inform and heighten the awareness of the public through social communication, the publication of work, a documentation centre and a specialist library;

(g) to take a position on questions which affect the equality of rights and opportunities, the situation of women and the reconciliation of family and professional responsibilities;

(h) to facilitate access to law, through a legal information service directed at women;

(i) to carry out specific projects, referred to in the objectives of the Commission, especially with the technical and/or financial support of international or national organizations;

(j) to co-operate with international organizations and foreign organizations which pursue similar objectives to those of the Commission, with a view to contributing to major international guidelines relating to equality and adopting them at a national level;

...

(l) to carry out or to support any other activities which contribute to the objectives of the Commission.

2. The Commission shall be consulted concerning all draft legal texts which relating to the problems of women and equality.

3. The Commission shall present an annual report of activities which have been carried out, resulting from its tasks.

7.4.4 DECREE (DL) NO 451/91 OF 4 DECEMBER 1991[1]

Under this Decree, the Commission for Equality and the Rights of Women was integrated into the Ministry of Employment and Social Security.

---

1 D.R., 1st series, 4 December 1991.

7.4.5 DECREE (DL) NO 496/77 OF 25 NOVEMBER 1977[1]

This text amends various articles of the Civil Code, including the following:

Article 1671 – Equality of a married couple

1. Marriage is based on the equality of rights and duties of the couple.

...

Article 1677-D – Exercising a profession or other activity

Each partner may exercise a profession or any activity whatsoever without the consent of the other partner.

7.4.6 DECREE (DL) NO 330/90 OF 23 OCTOBER 1990[2]

Article 7 – Principle of adherence to constitutionality

1. Any publicity which, by its form, objective or aim, contravenes the values, institutions and fundamental principles of the Constitution is prohibited.
2. In particular, the prohibition covers publicity which: ...

(d) contains discrimination based on race or sex.

...

1 D.R., 1st series, 25 November 1977.
2 D.R., 1st series, 23 October 1990.

8. CASES

8.1 DECISIONS ON THE PRINCIPLE OF EQUALITY

Supreme Administrative Tribunal, 1 March 1990[1]
Caminhos de Ferro Portugueses EP contra Manuel Coutinho and others

The legal-constitutional content of the principle of equality encompasses the following areas: the prohibition of arbitrary action, the prohibition of discrimination, and the obligation to differentiate.

8.2 DECISIONS ON EQUAL PAY

Supreme Administrative Tribunal, 27 February 1973[2]

Given that cashier work is carried out exclusively by female staff, there is no place for a reduction in pay based on 'unequal conditions' in relation to work carried out by men.

Supreme Administrative Tribunal, 22 May 1973[3]
Estoril SARL contra Maria dos Anjos Vieira

I EQUAL PAY BETWEEN MALE AND FEMALE WORKERS FOR WORK OF EQUAL VALUE IS A PRINCIPLE PROVIDED FOR BY LAW.
II WOMEN AND MEN MUST RECEIVE EQUAL PAY WHEN THEY WORK AS LEVEL-CROSSING GUARDS.

The following facts arise from this case:

(a) The woman defendant entered the service of the plaintiffs on 22 June 1949;
(b) during this period, the plaintiffs employed both male and female staff to work as guards on level-crossings, their work consisting of ensuring the safety of the movement of trains, vehicles and pedestrians;
(c) ... from 1 August 1966, male level-crossing guards received monthly pay of 1,500 ESC, whereas women level-crossing guards received 900 ESC per month;
(d) ... from 1 October 1966, male level-crossing guards received monthly pay of 2,000 ESC, whereas women level-crossing guards received 1,050 ESC per month;

---

1 *Ac. Doutr.*, No 343, July 1990, p. 1017.
2 *Ac. Doutr.*, No 136, April 1973, p. 604.
3 *Ac. Doutr.*, No 140/141, August-September 1973, p. 1262.

(e) ... from 1 January 1970, male level-crossing guards received monthly pay of 2,050 ESC, whereas women level-crossing guards received 1,200 ESC per month;

...

According to this statement of facts, the plaintiffs employed both male and female staff as level-crossing guards, their work consisting of ensuring the safety of the movement of trains, vehicles and pedestrians; there were no objective differences between the work of men and women regarding the time allowed for work, its content, duration and efficiency.

This means that the work carried out by women as level-crossing guards is absolutely equal in all respects to that carried out by men carrying out the same functions.

The law in force at the time, art. 115(a) of Decree (DL) No 47302 of 4 November 1966, like the current law, art. 116(2) of Decree (DL) No 49408 of 24 November 1969, approving the legal framework of the contract of employment, introduced into our country the principle contained in Convention No 100 of the International Labour Organization, ... according to which there should be equal pay between male and female workers for work of equal value. ...

As the plaintiffs paid men more than they paid women, even though both groups were carrying out the same functions as level-crossing guards, the judge admitted the defendant's claim as lawful; for this reason, the appeal was rejected and the decision against *Estoril* regarding the payment of different pay was confirmed.

Supreme Court of Justice, 4 June 1981[1]
Estoril SARL contra Maria da Conceição Bráulio and others

I EQUAL PAY FOR MALE AND FEMALE WORKERS FOR WORK OF EQUAL VALUE IS A PRINCIPLE OF LAW.

II WOMEN LEVEL-CROSSING GUARDS MUST RECEIVE REMUNERATION EQUAL TO THAT PAID TO POINTS OPERATORS (WHICH IS HIGHER) WHO HAVE ALWAYS CARRIED OUT AND WILL CONTINUE EXCLUSIVELY TO CARRY OUT THE FUNCTIONS OF A LEVEL-CROSSING GUARD.

1. ...

(b) The duties of the women defendants consisted of ... guarding level-crossings.

(c) During the years prior to 1 April 1974, the afore-mentioned functions were carried out in the plaintiff company, by men and by women,

1 *Supremo Tribunal de Justiça, Ac. Doutr.*, No 235, July 1981, p. 954.

without distinction and as their exclusive duty, in the job category of 'operator'.

(d) The plaintiffs, who previously had paid higher remuneration to men than to women for the afore-mentioned duties, raised the pay of the latter to the level of that of the men, after this was decreed in law;[1] they maintained this attitude until March 1974, inclusive.

(e) On 1 April 1974 the plaintiffs classified as 'points operators' male workers who exclusively carried out the duties of level-crossing guards and who previously had been employed as such; in fact, these workers continued to carry out the same tasks.

(f) Several months later, the plaintiffs tried to place these men in positions where they were carrying out the functions of 'points operators' and, to this end, subjected them to a medical examination. As a result of this examination, it became apparent that the men did not have the required level of health ... and the plaintiffs therefore kept them in the duties which they had always carried out: as 'level-crossing guards', which required less physical effort.

(g) The pay of male workers who had always carried out the duties of 'level-crossing guards' was as follows: from 1 April 1974: 3,520 ESC; from 1 June 1974: 5,093 ESC; finally, from 1 January 1975: 8,500 ESC.

(h) For the same periods, women level-crossing guards earned, respectively, 3,125 ESC, 3,630 ESC and 5,000 ESC.

(i) In April and December 1976, the plaintiffs took on several male workers in the category and function of 'level-crossing guard' and paid them a remuneration equal to that of women who carried out identical functions.

(j) The 'level-crossing guards' section is divided into three shifts working, respectively, from 8 am to 5 pm, from 3 pm to midnight, and from midnight to 9 am; women are employed only in the first two shifts, which deal with the heaviest traffic.

2. The judge of first instance rejected the application. ... However, the Court of Appeal (*Tribunal da Relação*) in Lisbon decided otherwise, ... overruling the decision taken at first instance.

...

4. ... The question here is to find out whether, in the present case, it is right to accept and to respect the legal principle according to which equal pay for male and female workers should be required for work ... of equal value.

... Article 116(1) and(2) of Decree (DL) No 49408 of 24 November 1969 ... provides that it is the duty of the employer to secure for women working conditions appropriate for their sex, especially ensuring the preservation of their health and morality and guaranteeing them the right to receive, for the same tasks, the same qualification and the same work rate, the same remuneration as men.

---

1 See the decision cited above, p. 81.

This means ... that our labour legislation ... is going in a direction which echoes the principle contained in Convention No 100 of the International Labour Organization, which institutes equal pay between male and female workers for work of equal value.

Moreover, the principle according to which there shall be 'equal pay for equal work' also features in art. 53(a) of the Constitution.[1] ...

It is in this sense that the decision of the Supreme Administrative Tribunal (*Supremo Tribunal Administrativo*) was taken on 22 May 1973. ...

Thus, and in the face of established facts, ... the decision which is the object of the appeal must be ... confirmed ..., given that the company Estoril has violated the principle of equality. ...

From now on, ... women defendants must be paid damages in the form of compensation for the amount they were under-paid in relation to their colleagues. ...

Lisbon Court of Appeal (Social Section), 26 November 1979[2]
Estoril SARL contra Maria da Conceição Bráulio and others

The facts described in the previous case apply here also. The decision is also the same. The following are some significant extracts:

In its submissions the respondents, *Estoril SARL*, maintained that the facts were not the same as those which had been used as a basis for the decision of the Supreme Administrative Tribunal of 22 May 1973 and those to which the present action refers; however, ... workers who 'had been employed as points operators continued to fulfil the role of level-crossing guards'. ...

As for the decision according to which the company had to transfer men who fulfilled the duties of level-crossing guards to the grade of operator and surveillance at another grade — that of maintenance, within the category of points operators — art. 25 of Decree (DRegul.) No 47472 of 31 December 1966 provided for the removal of the category of level-crossing operator (men) and their obligatory re-classification in a different category, with no loss of remuneration; however, it was proved, as we have said, that men continued to fulfil the duties of level-crossing guards.

1 Now art. 59(1)(a) of the Constitution.
2 BTE, 2nd series, Nos 10-12, 1984, p. 1125.

There is one single and evident reality: for a long time, men and women have been taken on by *Estoril* as level-crossing guards ... and will not cease to be so employed.

Clause 22 of the Collective Agreement of 1972, which until 31 December 1974 regulated ... changes in category and salary, implied that, until the day of actual taking up of a new position of employment, interested parties would remain in the former category, with the remuneration appropriate to this. ...

Neither is the argument accepted according to which these workers, not being qualified to carry out the duties of points operators, could be transferred to another position, the category and income of which would not be inferior. In reality, the *jus variandi* is only accepted if a request is made by the worker to carry out on a purely temporary basis different duties, with no change of category, from those for which he was employed, and then to return to the latter duties. ...

It is imperative therefore to pay equal pay for identical duties, the contrary being discriminatory and prohibited by art. 13(2) of the Constitution.

***Supreme Court of Justice, 24 October 1980*[1]**
Delfina Maria Mota and others contra Estoril SARL

This decision was the same as in the preceding case, involving similar facts.

***Lisbon Court of Appeal (Social Section), 12 July 1982*[2]**
Estoril SARL contra Maria Herminia Raposo

The facts of this case were similar to the preceding cases, and the decision was also the same. The following is an extract from the decision:

The fact that male guards always carry out their duties during the night shift does not in itself justify them being paid higher pay than that awarded to women guards, who always carry out their duties during the day shift; in fact, it has been shown that the day shifts deal with heavier traffic and the hours worked during the night are the only ones to benefit from remuneration with a statutory increase.[3]

---

1 Unreported.
2 BTE, 2nd series, Nos 7-9, 1986, p. 1009.
3 See also on this point the decision of 22 November 1982, cited below.

Lisbon Court of Appeal (Social Section), 22 November 1982[1]
Estoril SARL contra Victória Maria Rodrigues

The facts of this case were similar to the preceding cases, and the decision was also the same. The following is an extract from the decision:

Even more recently, Decree (DL) No 392/79 of 20 September 1979, in addressing this problem again, provided for the following rule in art. 9(1) relating to employment relations:

> Equal remuneration between male and female workers for equal work or for work of equal value carried out for the same employer shall be guaranteed.
>
> ...

As such, we cannot accept that male level-crossing guards carry out their duties only on the night shift, unlike the female guards who only work on day shifts. This is mainly because the day shifts deal with the heaviest traffic, and secondly, because the night hours are remunerated with a statutory bonus.

Lisbon Court of Appeal (Social Section), 12 October 1983[2]
Estoril SARL contra Mariana de Oliveira

The facts of this case were similar to the preceding cases, and the decision was also the same.

Lisbon Labour Tribunal, 3 July 1990[3]
Luisa Martins Rodrigues Pinto contra Certifix

... The facts of the case were as follows:

(a) The plaintiff has been working for the defendants ... since at least 1981.
(b) ... She earns 36,500 ESC per month by way of basic pay, with an additional sum of 150 ESC per day as a meal and travel allowance.

...

(d) For about eight years, all workers in the employment of the defendants have received an allowance for meals, initially fixed at 150 ESC; this amount is identical for all workers.
(e) In February 1988, the defendants modified the amounts of the allowances, with men subsequently receiving 400 ESC per day; this amount was later increased to 465 ESC.

---

1 BTE, 2nd series, Nos 10-12, 1985, p. 1318.
2 BTE, 2nd series, Nos 3-4, 1986, p. 384.
3 *Tribunal do Trabalho*, unreported.

(f) Women still received the same daily allowances: 150 ESC, except for a woman worker in the defendant's administration section, who began to receive the amounts indicated in the preceding paragraph.

...

(h) According to the collective agreement in force, the defendants were not obliged to pay meal allowances.

(i) The main activity of the defendants is in the high precision mechanical industry (design and manufacture of moulds).

(j) Given the highly technical nature of this activity, the workers who are employed there have a high degree of specialization and of expert knowledge.

(k) At the end of 1987 and the beginning of 1988, certain of the workers in the high precision mechanics sector asked the defendants for a pay increase , threatening to terminate their contracts.

(l) In order to avoid the consequences which the departure of these employees would have brought about, as it would have been difficult to replace them, the defendants agreed to increase the pay of all skilled workers.

(m) This was achieved by increasing the meal allowances paid to these workers, as suggested by the workers, as this allowance, added to pay, was not subject to tax and social insurance.

(n) The defendants have a grade in which women work, amongst them the plaintiff, ... [consisting of] work not requiring any skilled workers, and for which recruitment is easy.

(o) From January 1988, the defendants granted their workers, including the plaintiff and the other workers in the grade to which she belongs, a travel allowance, the amount of which was fixed for each worker according to their social insurance.

...

It is incumbent upon us to assess the soundness of the request.

... Article 2(c) of Decree (DL) No 392/79 of 20 September 1979 covers ... the meal allowance. However, the retrospective nature of the meal allowance cannot in any way allow us to lose sight of the object and *raison d'être* of such an allowance ... The meal allowance is not granted according to the work carried out or the professional category of the worker. ...

The same applies to the travel allowance paid by the defendants which, as we have seen, is calculated not according to the professional category of the worker or criteria of recruitment used in the labour market, but simply according to the type of subscription paid by each worker; this means that it does not depend on the different distances which the workers have to travel to get to and to return from their place of work.

More precisely, it is in consideration of the nature of the meal allowance that we cannot accept the defendants' argument regarding art. 9(4) of Decree (DL) No 392/79. The fact that there has been added to the allowance paid to the skilled workers an amount corresponding to the increase which they wanted does not overcome the fact that it is an allowance ...: the allowance is paid per number of working days.

Whatever the defendants' motive may be, ... when they added to the meal allowance the amount corresponding to an increase in pay, there was nothing to stop this amount ... henceforth being considered as an increase to the meal allowance granted to these skilled workers, who were all male. Therefore the company maintained a meal allowance of 150 ESC for unskilled female workers, who were all women, except for a fairly incomprehensible exception, which we referred to earlier. ...

... The plaintiff demonstrated that discrimination existed between the meal allowance she received herself and the meal allowance granted to male workers in the skilled section.

This discrimination exists because it does not concern basic pay, but rather an allowance the aim of which was stated earlier. For this reason the defendants' argument that the case does not involve equal work is not valid. We should repeat this. We are not concerned with such considerations in the granting of meal allowances.

Therefore, the tribunal considers the action to be sound and orders the defendant to pay the plaintiff a meal allowance identical to the one which is currently paid to skilled workers; it also orders, as requested, the defendants to back-date payment of this.

8.3 DECISIONS ON EQUAL TREATMENT

Coimbra Court of Appeal, 8 March 1988[1]

Manuel de Freitas Lopes e Cª, Ldª contra Maria de Fátima Cunha

I LIMITATIONS, PROHIBITIONS OF OR CONDITIONS REGARDING ACCESS FOR WOMEN TO EMPLOYMENT ARE ONLY LEGITIMATE IN SO FAR AS THEIR INTENTION IS TO AVOID ACTUAL OR POTENTIAL RISKS TO HEALTH.

II AS IT IS CONTRARY TO THE PRINCIPLE OF FREE ACCESS FOR WOMEN TO POSITIONS OF EMPLOYMENT WHICH INVOLVE THE USE OF DANGEROUS MACHINERY, ESPECIALLY CIRCULAR SAWS, ART. 78 OF THE SAFETY REGULATIONS FOR MECHANICAL WORK IN MADEIRA IS DEEMED TO BE ABROGATED.

III THERE IS THEREFORE NO FOUNDATION FOR ADDITIONS TO PENSIONS AND COMPENSATION PAID TO A WOMEN WORKER INJURED BY A CIRCULAR SAW WITH WHICH SHE WAS WORKING, GIVEN THAT THE ACCIDENT CAN NO LONGER BE CONSIDERED AS BEING THE RESULT OF A FAILURE OF THE EMPLOYER TO OBSERVE A PRINCIPLE OF LAW.

Maria de Fátima Cunha brought an action before the Labour Tribunal ... against the insurance company Bonança EP and the company Manuel Freitas Lopes e Cª, Lᵈᵃ, requesting that they be required to pay her sums ... in compensation for an accident which she suffered on 19 May 1980 while she was working with a circular saw under the authority, direction and supervision of the company named Manuel de Freitas Lopes e Cª, Lᵈᵃ, which had concluded an insurance contract with the aforementioned company covering accidents at work.

... The judge ... ordered Manuel de Freitas Lopes ... [as well as] the insurance company Bonança EP to pay the sums claimed by the plaintiff.

The company appealed.

... The facts:

(a) On 19 May 1980, while she was working under the authority, direction and supervision of the afore-mentioned company, as well as on their behalf, ... Maria de Fátima Cunha suffered an accident.
(b) This accident involved the person in question being injured by a circular saw with which she working at the time.
(c) The company had placed the worker in the category of 'unclassified'.
(d) As such, it was the responsibility of the worker to transport, load and unload all materials and to clean the work area, as well as to tidy and pile up wood, and, sometimes, to cut off points with a circular saw.

---

1 *Col. Jurisp.*, Coimbra, 13th year, Book II, 1988, p. 106.

(e) The insurance company, Bonança EP, accepted the transfer of responsibility relating to the monthly pay of 7,500 ESC, as augmented by the holiday allowance and the Christmas allowance for the same amount.

...

According to the conclusions of the appellants, they were, first, opposed to the additions to the pension and compensation imposed by the first judge, ...; the latter decided that the accident was the result of a fault on the part of the employer, due to failure to observe a legal provision, art. 78 of the Safety Regulations for the Mechanical Industry in Madeira. Moreover, the appellants contested their responsibility for these payments, given the insurance contract concluded with the insurance company, Bonança EP ...

Article 78, mentioned above, provides that 'work by women and children of less than 10 years of age involving the use of dangerous machinery, especially ... circular saws ...', is prohibited.

However, art. 4 of Decree (DL) No 392/79 of 20 September 1979 provides in para. 1 that 'access for women to all employments, professions or positions of employment shall be guaranteed', and it adds in para. 2 that, apart from what is contained in art. 8, 'all statutory and regulatory provisions ... which, in some way, limit the access of women to any employment, profession or position of employment' are to be considered as 'invalid and without effect'. Article 8 in turn states that 'work which, according to the law, is considered to involve an actual or potential risk to the genetic system shall be prohibited or subjected to conditions'.

Moreover, art. 23 of Decree (DL) No 392/79 provides that 'all statutory, regulatory and administrative provisions contrary to the principle of free access for women to all employments, professions or positions of employment, including those which refer to criteria of selection, regardless of the sector or branch of activity, at all levels of the professional hierarchy, are repealed'.

In the light of the provisions of Decree (DL) No 392/79, we should consider art. 78 of the afore-mentioned regulations as repealed, since it prevents access for women to positions of employment which would involve the use of dangerous machinery, especially circular saws.

This legal text seeks to introduce legal standards transposing certain constitutional principles to the real world and to labour law; it establishes mechanisms for action which would render possible the practical application of these standards and principles.

One of the constitutional principles which constitutes one of the most important pillars of our legal order is the principle of equality, contained in art. 13 of the Constitution of the Republic of Portugal; one of the most significant manifestations of it is equality in access to employment. By virtue of this principle, all discrimination in access to employment based on sex is unlawful (art. 13(2) of the Constitution).

However, the Constitution does not confine itself to protecting a general principle of equality. It requires the State, in matters of access to employment and in order to guarantee a right to work, to ensure 'equality of opportunity in the choice of profession or type of work, as well as the conditions of work, in order that access to any office, work or professional category is not closed or limited on the basis of sex' (art. 58(3)(b) of the Constitution).[1]

In this provision, the Constitution reinforces the principle of equality, from which originated the prohibition of discrimination based on sex in access to duties, to work or to professional categories. 'With this Constitutional injunction for State action, the aim was, in practice, to eliminate inequality of opportunities for women. It gave effective content to one of the components of freedom of choice of profession, and, by means of this, to the right to work.' (GOMES CANTILHO AND VITAL MOREIRA, *Constituiçao da República Portuguesa Anotada*, Coimbra, vol. 1, 2nd edition., p. 320).

However, freedom of professional choice and equality in access to employment are not incompatible with certain restrictions. This is so in particular in relation to the prohibition of certain work for minors and women and its being subjected to conditions. These restrictions are legitimate if they aim to protect the physical and psychological development of minors (art. 60(2)(c) of the Constitution)[2] or the genetic system of women (art. 8(1) of the Constitution).

This is why we can conclude that the limitations and prohibitions applying to access of women to employment or making this access subject to certain conditions are only legitimate in so far as they aim to avoid 'actual or potential risks to the genetic system'; they are not thus when they can be justified by other ends, ...

Article 78 of the afore-mentioned regulations did not aim to avoid risks to the genetic system of women, but only to contribute to the reduction in accidents at work by taking into consideration the physical faculties of women and the characteristics of the machines used for working with wood. These machines expose their operators to higher risks, given their inherent danger, and cause a large number of occupational accidents. ...

1 Now art. 58(3)(b) of the Constitution.
2 Now art. 59(2)(c) of the Constitution.

Consequently, art. 78 must be considered as repealed by the afore-mentioned provisions of Decree (DL) No 392/79, for the reason that it is contrary to free access for women to all employment, professions or positions of employment, given that it prevents their access to positions of employment which involve the use of dangerous machinery, especially circular saws.

However, the non-conformity of the said art. 78, together with the afore-mentioned principles taken from the Constitution, is obvious. However, it should still be considered as being materially unconstitutional and, consequently, invalid. ...

In fact, the collective agreement makes express provision for the category of circular saw operator, ... If art. 78 was in force, women would not be admitted to this professional category and to respective positions of employment, which would radically contradict the afore-mentioned provisions of the Constitution and Decree (DL) No 392/79.

Article 78 being invalid, there is no longer any basis for raising the pension and the compensation granted to Maria de Fátima Cunha, ... given that the accident can no longer be considered as being the result of a fault on the part of the employer, due to failure to observe a legal precept. ...

On the other hand, the insurer can no longer participate merely in a subsidiary role in relation to the payments normally provided for in the law and to which Maria de Fátima Cunha has a right. ... As it was obligatory for the company to transfer its responsibility to the insurance company Bonança EP, it is discharged of all responsibility. ...

Consequently, the judgment was dismissed and the appeal declared justified.

8.4 DECISIONS ON EQUALITY IN SOCIAL SECURITY

Constitutional Commission, 20 July 1980[1]
Public Ministry contra Portugal Previdente SARL

THE PROVISION CONTAINED IN PARA. 1(b) OF CHAPTER XIX OF LAW NO 2127 OF 3 AUGUST 1965, ACCORDING TO WHICH THE PENSION PAID TO A WIDOWER OF LESS THAN 65 YEARS OF AGE AND SUFFERING FROM AN ILLNESS WHICH CONSIDERABLY REDUCES HIS CAPACITY FOR WORK, SHALL BE 30 PER CENT OF THE BASIC REMUNERATION OF THE VICTIM (HIS WIFE), IS PARTIALLY UNCONSTITUTIONAL. THIS UNCONSTITUTIONALITY IS DUE TO THE VIOLATION OF THE PRINCIPLE OF EQUALITY GUARANTEED IN ART. 13(2) OF THE CONSTITUTION.

...

1. Joaquim da Rocha Maciel, aged less than 65 years and suffering from a physical incapacity to work in excess of 75 per cent, brought an action before the Labour Tribunal in Barcelos against the insurance company, Portugal Previdente. The tribunal decided that the plaintiff had the right to an annual pension corresponding to 40 per cent of the basic remuneration of the deceased victim ..., his wife. It thus concluded, on the one hand, that para. 1(b) of Chapter XIX of Law No 2127, in establishing an unjustified discriminatory framework in the event of widowhood, was violating art. 13(2) of the Constitution and, on the other hand, that the situation ought to be subject to para. 1(a) of the same Chapter XIX.

The Public Ministry appealed the question of unconstitutionality to the Constitutional Commission. ...

2. ... *Prima facie*, we should determine whether or not all of para. 1(b) of Chapter XIX of Law No 2127 is unconstitutional. ...

... The tribunal only considered the section according to which the pension paid to a widower aged less than 65 years and suffering from a physical illness which considerably reduces his capacity for work is 30 per cent of the basic remuneration of the deceased victim, his wife. ...

3. The constitutional principle with which this part of the provision comes into conflict ... is the principle of equality, based on art. 13 of the Constitution, particularly the prohibition of any discrimination based on sex (art. 13(2) of the Constitution).

An analysis of this kind firstly demands detailed work comparing para. 1(a) and (b) of the said Chapter XIX. ... These provisions may be subdivided into several sub-groups. ... Only one comparison between the two

---

1 *Comissão Constitucional*, BMJ, No 321, 1982, p. 231.

will allow the identification of the specific points of each of the regulations. ...

Sub-group 1:

(a) Up to the age of 65, a widow not suffering from a physical or mental illness which reduces her capacity to work ... by more than 75 per cent shall receive an annual pension corresponding to 30 per cent of the basic remuneration of the victim, her husband (sub-para. (a)) ...;

(b) Up to the age of 65, a widower not suffering from a physical or mental illness of this severity shall receive no pension (sub-para. (b)). ...

Sub-group 2:

(a) Up to the age of 65, a widow suffering from a physical or mental illness of this severity shall receive an annual pension corresponding to 40 per cent of the basic remuneration of the victim, her husband (sub-para. (a)) ...;

(b) Up to the age of 65, a widower suffering from an identical physical or mental illness shall receive a pension corresponding to 30 per cent of the basic remuneration of the victim, his wife (sub-para. (b)). ...

Sub-group 3:

(a) A widow aged over 65, whether or not she is suffering from such a physical or mental illness, shall receive a pension corresponding to 40 per cent of the basic remuneration of the victim, her husband (sub-para. (a)) ...;

(b) A widower aged over 65, whether or not he is suffering from an identical physical or mental illness, shall receive a pension corresponding to 30 per cent of the basic remuneration of the victim, his wife (sub-para. (b)). ...

Sub-group 4:

(a) A widow who remarries shall receive in one single payment an amount equal to three times the annual pension and shall, at the same time, lose her future right to the pension (sub-para. (a)) ...;

(b) A widower who abandons his state of widowhood shall lose his future right to the pension (sub-para. (b)). ...

Sub-group 5:

(a) A widow who engages in scandalous conduct will lose her right to the pension (sub-para. (a)) ...;

(b) A widow who engages in bad conduct will not lose his right to the pension (sub-para. (b)). ...

It is obviously not our responsibility to declare the whole of this multiple scheme unconstitutional. ... That does not mean that the Constitutional Commission cannot, for the purposes of analysis and evaluation, study the whole of the scheme relating to the right of surviving partners to the pension, for members of both sexes who were already married to the victim at the time of the accident at work. In reality, only an overall comparative examination will allow us to conclude that there was perhaps a violation of the principle of equality by the party in para. 1(b) of Chapter XIX of Law No 2127. ...

4. ... The constitutional equality principle requires equality in law and in fact, not merely formal equality. ... The equality principle demands ... that the legislature, in seeking to eliminate unequal practices which affect certain categories of citizens, creates positive discrimination in their favour, thereby remedying different and unjust situations within the political society in which the citizens live. It is in this way that we shall achieve real and substantial equality.

Consequently, the distinct regulation contained in para. 1(a) and (b) of Chapter XIX of Law No 2127, aimed at widows and widowers who already have a right to a pension due to death following an accident at work of the respective partners, cannot be considered as violating the principle of equality, a general principle affirmed in art. 13(1) of the Constitution.

What should be considered fundamentally is whether or not this differentiation based on sex can be justified: the causes or reasons listed in art. 13(2) may demand normative diversification, due to particular conditions, while still respecting the equality principle. ...

> Inequalities which have a sufficient material foundation must be accepted, and those which, in the absence of such foundation, prove to be truly arbitrary must be rejected.

5. Reasons for differentiation based on sex originate from the complex provisions contained in para. 1(a) and (b) of Chapter XIX of Law No 2127.

We shall pay no more attention to the fifth sub-group, ... as it is completely unrelated to the question with which we are concerned.

The guiding principle of the legal differences in the first four sub-groups resides in the fact that a widow has of her own account almost always less income than a widower. It therefore seemed fair to grant her a pension in the event of the widower not being able to benefit from it and to grant her more when the widower also benefited from it. But does this actually reflect reality?

We do not claim that all differentiations, of whatever nature, in the granting of a pension to surviving partners must be constitutionally unsound. To do so would be to say that it would not be so if it followed parameters which rigorously identified the economically weaker surviving partners.

Favourable treatment of the latter in the granting of pensions would thus be an objective and reasonable motivation.

Distinctions such as those found in para. 1(a) and (b) of Chapter XIX of Law No 2127, at least as far as the second sub-group are concerned, are based solely on the sex of the surviving partners and are today outdated with reference to social and legal reality. We should acknowledge that in the past, following a long tradition of discrimination, the majority of women in Portugal worked at home; a few worked outside the home and so earned a wage, generally less than that paid to men, even for identical jobs. It is also true that this situation has evolved. ... Existing differentiations are tending to disappear. Here we should highlight Decree (DL) No 392/79 of 20 September 1979 (the law on equality at work), which seeks to prevent all situations of discrimination between men and women at work: it particularly guarantees access for women to all jobs, professions or positions of employment (art. 4(1)); it guarantees women workers, in each company and in the same position, the right to pay equal to that of male workers (art. 9(1)); and it guarantees women workers access to the highest levels of the hierarchy in their profession (art. 10(1)).

All this shows that the position of women in the labour market today is still not equal to that of men, but also that we are advancing progressively towards perfect equality. ...

Distinctions in the right to the pension of surviving partners ... based solely on sex ... are, today, unreasonable, arbitrary and disproportionate, and are so for several reasons. First, this difference (between the situation of men and women) tends to be less and less accentuated. Next, a widower, like a widow, may fall into the category of the economically weakest surviving partners, for reasons which have nothing to do with sex. Finally, widowhood caused by the accidental death of the other partner may happen to anyone at any time during marriage: a wife who survives may be very young (between 25 and 29 years, when the employment of women reaches its highest level), or the survivor may have reached old age (when the rate of activity by women is at its lowest).

... Inequalities which persist in the labour market cannot be compensated for by new inequalities. ... We need to abolish the inequalities, but never by compensation. ...

As was written in the report of 9 February 1981 by the Commission of the European Communities addressed to the Council:

> The Commission is aware that progress in the direction of equality does not depend solely on the improvement of legal standards, but also on the evolution of attitudes, as it specified moreover in its memorandum of 1975, which, at the time, accompanied a proposal for a Directive. These legal standards, however, play an important role, in the sense that they bring about changes in attitudes.

In the same way, in the report on Decree (DL) No 392/79 cited above, we read:

> ... Equality as guaranteed in the Constitution will not be achieved through a simple implementation of law, given the depth of social, economic and political roots of discrimination against women.

Distinctions in the right of widows and widowers to pensions today can only imply a vague sense of compensation, and such compensation is to be condemned, as we have seen.

The maintenance of these distinctions ... would cause regression or paralysis of attitudes, which have already begun to accept equal treatment of all human beings in law, independent of their sex. This aspect, therefore, is no less relevant, especially in the context of a Constitution which, in art. 52(c)[1], gives the State the responsibility of guaranteeing on the one hand, by means of the application of economic and social policy plans, the right to work ensuring equality of opportunity in the choice of profession or type of work, and on the other hand, the assurance that access to all positions, work or professional categories is not prevented or restricted on grounds of sex.

We can conclude from all this that the second sub-group at least ... violates the principle of equality affirmed specifically in art. 13(2) of the Constitution. ...

6. The decision which is the object of this appeal is thus confirmed, where it declared unconstitutional the relevant part of para. 1(b) of Chapter XIX of Law No 2127 of 3 August 1965.

Constitutional Tribunal (2nd section), 20 May 1987[2]
Public Ministry contra Companhia de Seguros Tranquilidade EP

This decision is similar to the preceding case.

Constitutional Tribunal (2nd section), 18 November 1987[3]
Public Ministry contra Portugal Previdente SARL

This decision is similar to that of 20 July 1980.

---

1 Now art. 58(3)(c) of the Constitution.

2 *Tribunal Constitucional*, BMJ, No 367, 1987, p. 273.

3 D.R., 2nd series, No 41, 19 February 1988, p. 1622

Constitutional Tribunal, 20 September 1989[1]

For reasons similar to those in the decision of 20 July 1980, the tribunal annuls para. 1(b) of Chapter XIX of Law No 2127.

1 D.R., 2nd series, No 231, 6 October 1989, p. 4078.

9. DOCUMENTATION

9.1 BIBLIOGRAPHY

9.1.1 BOOKS

APELLES CONCEIÇÃO, M., *Segurança Social*, Lisbon, 1990.

CUVELLIER, R., *Employment and basic needs in Portugal*, Geneva, ILO, 1979.

GOMES CANOTILHO, J. J. and VITAL MOREIRA, M., *Constituição da República Portuguesa Anotada*, Coimbra, Coimbra Editora, 1991.

GOMES CANOTILHO, J.J., *Direito Constitucional*, Coimbra, Almedina, 1991.

LEITE, J. and ALMEIDA, F., *Legislação do trabalho*, 5th ed., Coimbra, Coimbra Editora, November 1991.

MIRANDA, J., *Manual de Direito Constitucional*, Book IV ('Direitos Fundamentais'), Coimbra, Coimbra Editora, 1988.

MOTA DE CAMPOS, J., *Direito Comunitário*, vol. II, 3rd ed., Lisbon, Fundação Calouste Gulbenkian, 1990.

VON PRONDZYNSKI, F., *Implementation of the Equality Directives*, Luxembourg, Commission of the European Communities, 1987.

Regimes Portugueses de Segurança Social, Secretaria de Estado da Segurança Social, Lisbon, Departamento de Relações Internacionais e Convenções de Segurança Social, 1988.

9.1.2 ARTICLES, NOTES AND REPORTS

A. F. C., 'Mulheres: o gosto de intervir', *Emprego e Formação*, No 7, January 1989, p. 95.

ALMEIDA, A.,

— 'Trabalho feminino e estratégias familiares', *Análise Social*, No 85, 1985, p. 7.
— 'Entre o dizer e o fazer: a construção da identidade feminina', *Análise Social*, Nos 92-93, 1986, p. 493.
— 'Um universo feminino: as donas de casa e o trabalho doméstico', *Educação e Trabalho*, No 32, 1984, p. 28.
— 'Mulheres, Trabalho e Família', *A mulher na sociedade portuguesa: visão histórica e perspectivas actuais*, Coimbra, IHES/FLUC, vol. I, 1986, p. 421.

ALMEIDA, H., *Factores determinantes das diferenciações salariais interindústrias*, Lisbon, Ministério do Trabalho, 1974.

AMÂNCIO, L. and LIMA, M. L., *Inquérito Nacional sobre Assédio Sexual no Mercado de Trabalho*, trabalho encomendado pela CITE ao Centro de Investigação e Estudos de Sociologia do ISCTE, July 1989.

ANTUNES, V.,

— 'Projecto de estrutura orgânica do sistema nacional de inspecção do trabalho', *Revista da Administração Pública*, No 15, January-March 1982, p. 1323.
— 'Normalização do Relatório periódico da Inspecção do Trabalho', *Revista da Administração Pública*, No 13, July-September 1981, p. 473.

BAÇÃO, M. L., *Segurança social e protecção da maternidade em Portugal*, Lisbon, Comissão da Condição Feminina (caderno No 22), 1987, p. 121.

BARROS, A. and MENDES, F., 'Formas de produção e estatutos de trabalho na agricultura portuguesa', *Boletim da Sociedade de Geografia de Lisboa*, Nos 7-12, 1975, p. 169.

BELEZA, L.,
— 'A Convenção sobre a eliminação de todas as formas de Discriminação contra as Mulheres — Comentário', *Boletim da Comissão da Condição Feminina*, No 1, January-March 1980, p. 47.
— 'O Direito da Família na Constituição', *Boletim da Comissão da Condição Feminina*, No 4, October-December 1980, p. 7.
— 'O Estatuto das Mulheres na Constituição', *Estudos sobre a Constituição*, vol. I, Lisbon, Livraria Petrony, 1977, p. 63.
— 'A reforma do Código Civil e a situação legal das mulheres', *Boletim da Comissão da Condição Feminina*, No 10, 1977, p. 3.

BOTÃO, M. A.,
— *Assédio sexual no Local de Trabalho*, *Comissão da Condição Feminina* (Colecção 'Informar as mulheres', No 11), Lisbon, 1989.
— *Guia dos Direitos das Mulheres*, *Comissão da Condição Feminina* (Colecção 'Informar as mulheres', No 10), Lisbon, 1989, p. 52.

BOTELHO MONIZ, C., 'L'égalité juridique entre hommes et femmes en droit portugais', in VERWILGHEN, M. (ed.), *Equality in Law between Men and Women in the European Community*, vol. 2, Louvain-la-Neuve, Presses Universitaires de Louvain, 1986, p. 335.

CANCO, D., 'Alguns números sobre a participação da mulher na vida profissional (1974, 1981)', *Boletim da Comissão da Condição Feminina*, Nos 2-3, September 1983, p. 39.

CARRILHO, M., *As Mulheres e a Defesa Nacional — Elementos para a perspectivação de uma política aplicada a Portugal*, Comissão da Condição Feminina (caderno No 30), 1989.

CHABAUD, J., 'A educação mundial: imperativo mundial', *Educação e Trabalho*, No 10, 1979, p. 35.

COMISSÃO PARA A IGUALDADE NO TRABALHO E NO EMPREGO,
— *Pareceres: 1989-1991*, Lisbon, 1992.
— *Plano de actividades*, Lisbon, 1991.

COMISSÃO DA CONDIÇÃO FEMININA (CFF),
— 'A integração de Portugal na Comunidade Económica Europeia e estatuto das mulheres', *Boletim da Comissão da Condição Feminina*, No 7, 1977, p. 9.
— 'Mulheres Polícias: igualdade de oportunidades', *Boletim da Comissão da Condição Feminina*, No 2, April-June 1981, p. 65.

COMISSÃO CONSTITUCIONAL,
— 'Parecer No 28/81', *Boletim do Ministério da Justiça*, No 314, 1982, p. 65.
— 'Parecer No 33/81', *Boletim do Ministério da Justiça*, No 314, 1982, p. 82.

CORMELLI, M. E., 'Discriminação da mulher no trabalho e no emprego', *A mulher na sociedade portuguesa: visão histórica e perspectivas actuais*, vol. I, Coimbra, IHES/FLUC, 1986, p. 397.

DEPARTAMENTO CENTRAL DE PLANEAMENTO, 'A situação económica portuguesa e os seus desequilíbrios espaciais', *Planeamento*, vol. 7, No 3, 1985, p. 129.

FERREIRA, V., 'Mulheres, família e trabalho doméstico no capitalismo', *Revista crítica de Ciências Sociais*, No 6, May 1981, p. 47.

FONSECA, A.,
— 'A discriminação contra as mulheres existe? Sim ou Não?', *Boletim da Comissão da Condição Feminina*, March 1979, p. 7.
— 'Formação profissional: um caminho para a igualdade de oportunidades', *Boletim da Comissão da Condição Feminina*, No 2, June 1982, p. 39.
— 'OCDE — O papel das mulheres na economia', *Boletim da Comissão da Condição Feminina*, No 7, 1977, p. 27.
— 'Organização do tempo de trabalho', *Boletim da Comissão da Condição Feminina*, No 1, March 1980, p. 19.

GAUSSIN, J., 'Novas tecnologias e trabalho feminino', *Análise Psicológica*, series II, Nos 2-3, 1982, p. 225.

GOMES, B., 'Doze anos de democracia em Portugal: o papel das mulheres', *Desenvolvimento*, No 3, October 1986, p. 87.

LEAL, I., 'As mulheres na nova Constituição Portuguesa', *Boletim da Comissão da Condição Feminina*, No 3, January-March 1976, p. 1.

LEITUA, M. J. and CAMPOS, M. F., 'A mulher e o trabalho rural', *Vida rural*, No 3, July 1976, p. 10.

LEMOS, M. A.,
— 'Problemas relativos à Ratificação e Revisão da Convenção n.° 104 da OIT sobre Protecção da Maternidade', *Boletim da Comissão da Condição Feminina*, No 2, April-June 1982, p. 3.
— 'Considerações acerca do Relatório de Portugal sobre a execução da Convenção para a eliminação da discriminação contra as mulheres', *Boletim da Comissão da Condição Feminina*, No 1, 1983, p. 36.

LIMA, M., *Alguns aspectos simbólicos do poder da mulher*, Comissão da Condição Feminina (caderno No 20), 1987, p. 41.

LOPES, L., 'A mulher e o direito ao trabalho', *Fronteira*, No 4, October 1988.

LOPES, M. E., 'O estatuto e a carreira da mulher investigadora nos institutos e laboratórios do Estado', Comissão da Condição Feminina (caderno No 21), 1987, p. 169.

MONTEIRO, J. A., 'Higiene do trabalho: alguns aspectos', *Revista Técnica do Trabalho*, No 3, March 1980, p. 69.

MOURA, H., 'O difícil accesso à génese das aspirações sociais', *Psicologia*, vol. V, No 2, 1987, p. 189.

NUNES, M. C.,
— 'A mulher no emprego em Portugal', *Boletim da Comissão da Condição Feminina*, No 1, January-March 1979, p. 19.
— 'A mulher entre a família e o trabalho', *Economia e Socialismo*, No 63, December 1984, p. 71.
— 'Ensino e Emprego de Mulheres', *Cadernos de Consulta Psicológica*, No 1, 1985, p. 77.

— 'Formação de mulheres em áreas não tradicionais', *Emprego e Formação*, No 5, May 1988, p. 49.

NUNES, M. C., ABRANTES, B. and PRETO, J., 'A discriminação da mulher nos anúncios de oferta de emprego', *Boletim da Comissão da Condição Feminina*, Nos 3-4, 1984, p. 45.

OLIVEIRA, J., 'Mercado de trabalho, "Dualismo" e acções colectivas', *Revista crítica de Ciências Sociais*, Nos 15-16-17, May 1985, p. 397.

PIMENTA, C., 'Os salários profissionais líder: o caso português', *Revista Técnica do Trabalho*, Nos 14-16, September 1984, p. 181.

PROCURADORIA-GERAL DA REPÚBLICA,
— 'Parecer No 134/77', *Boletim do Ministério da Justiça*, No 278, 1978, p. 24.
— 'Parecer No 103/82', *Boletim do Ministério da Justiça*, No 326, 1983, p. 244.
— 'Parecer No 56/86', *Boletim do Ministério da Justiça*, No 360, 1986, p. 293.

PSACHAROPOULOS, G., *A educação e a estrutura de salários em Portugal*, Gabinete de Estudos e Planeamento do Ministério da Educação e Ciência, Lisbon, 1981.

REIL, L. and ALMEIDA, A., 'Papéis e tarefas familiares: comentários a um inquérito', *Alter Ego*, No 3, 1987, p. 47.

RIBEIRO, M. E.,
— *Tentativa de avaliação do impacto das despesas, no domínio do mercado de trabalho, relativamente às mulheres (1982 a 1986)*, December 1987.
— *Os trabalhadores de baixos salários no mercado de emprego em Portugal*, Direcção de Estudos e Planeamento do Ministério do Trabalho (Colecção Estudos, No 47), Lisbon, 1980.

ROCHA, A., 'A mulher na vida sindical', *Educação e Trabalho*, No 7, 1978, Lisbon, p. 21.

ROCHA, E., 'Nota sobre a população activa agrícola segundo o Recenseamento e segundo o Inquérito permanente ao Emprego: em busca de 300 000 mulheres', *Análise Social*, No 84, 1984, p. 701.

RODRIGO, I.,
— 'As estatísticas e o trabalho feminino', *Estudos de economia*, vol. 5, No 3, 1985, p. 321.
— 'Feminização da agricultura', *Análise Social*, Nos 92-93, p. 643.
— *As mulheres agricultoras, as transformações recentes na agricultura e a formação profissional*, Comissão da Condição Feminina (caderno No 22), 1987, p. 157.

RODRIGUES, J., 'Continuidade e mudança nos papéis das mulheres urbanas portuguesas: emergência de novas estruturas familiares', *Análise Social*, Nos 77-78-79, 1983, p. 909.

ROMÃO, I., *Papéis sexuais e formação técnica — A influência do sistema de ensino*, Comissão da Condição Feminina (caderno No 21), 1987, p. 251.

RUIVO, B., 'A mulher poder profissional: a mulher em actividades de investigação científica em Portugal', *Análise Social*, Nos 92-93, 1986, p. 669.

SANCHES, A., 'Mercado de trabalho e segmentação do Mercado de trabalho: algumas reflexões', *Economia e socialismo*, No 62, 1984, p. 89.

SANTANA, M. O., 'A Mulher no Trabalho', *Sindicato dos Quadros Técnicos do Estado*, 2nd year, Series II, No 2, March-April 1990, p. 2.

SILVA, M.,
— *O Emprego das Mulheres em Portugal*, Lisbon, Afrontamento, 1983.
— *A Igualdade de Oportunidades de Formação Profissional para as Mulheres*, Lisbon, Comissão da Condição Feminina (caderno No 17), 1983.
— *Trabalho e emprego das mulheres em Portugal*, Lisbon, Comissão para a Igualdade no Trabalho e no Emprego, 1982.

SOUSA, C. and PINTO, M. R., 'O trabalho feminino na sociedade', *A Ideia*, Nos 34-35, 1984, p. 100.

TAVARES DA SILVA, M. R., 'Publicidade e igualdade entre mulheres e homens', *Boletim da Comissão da Condição Feminina*, Nos 2-3, 1983, p. 68.

TRIGO, M. M., *A mulher como quadro-superior na implementação dos novas tecnologias*, Comissão da Condição Feminina (caderno No 21), 1987, p. 287.

VALENTE, M. O. and BARRIOS, A., 'Que razões levam os alunos à frequência dos cursos de formação de professores', *Revista de Educação*, No 1, December 1986, p. 13.

VERMELHO, L., 'A discriminação entre homens e mulheres: análise das convenções colectivas, 1980', *Boletim da Comissão da Condição Feminina*, No 4, October-December 1981, p. 5.

VIEGAS, L., *A Constituição e a Condição da Mulher*, Lisbon, Diabril, 1977.

WALL, K., 'O trabalho da mulher na emigração', *Educação e Trabalho*, No 32, 1984, p. 43.

Acções Positivas, uma aposta para a igualdade de oportunidades entre mulheres e homens — Actas de um seminário, Lisbon, Comissão da Condição Feminina (caderno n.° 28), 1989.

Anuário de Estatísticas Sociais — Portugal e Continente, Lisbon, Ministério do Emprego e da Segurança Social, Departamento de Estatística, 1991.

'CEE: Oportunidades iguais para as trabalhadoras', *Boletim da Comissão da Condição Feminina*, No 2, April-June 1980, p. 5.

O Direito Comunitário e a Igualdade Jurídica entre Mulheres e Homens — Comunicações de um Seminário, Lisbon, Comissão da Condição Feminina (caderno n.° 23), 1987.

O Direito Comunitário e as Mulheres, Bruxelles, Comissão das Comunidades Europeias (Mulheres da Europa, suppl. No 25), 1987

'Direito das mães trabalhadoras', *Boletim da Comissão da Condição Feminina*, No 2, April-June 1979, p. 19.

'Discriminações contra as mulheres no trabalho', *Boletim da Comissão da Condição Feminina*, No 5, July-September 1976, p. 1.

'Discriminações salariais contra as trabalhadoras portuguesas e remunerações praticadas', *Boletim da Comissão da Condição Feminina*, No 8, April-June 1977, p. 8.

Estratégias para o Futuro: progresso das mulheres até ao ano 2000, Lisbon, Comissão da Condição Feminina, 1989.

Inquérito ao emprego, Ministério do Emprego e da Segurança Social, Departamento de Estatística, January 1989.

Inquérito aos ganhos, Ministério do Emprego e da Segurança Social, Departamento de Estatística, April 1989, April 1991.

A Mulher e o Ensino Superior, a Investigação Científica e as Novas Tecnologias em Portugal — Actas de um Seminário (1987), Lisbon, Comissão da Condição Feminina (caderno No 21), 1987.

As mulheres trabalhadoras, Terceira Conferência Sindical, 10-11 April 1992.

Portugal — Situação das Mulheres — 1991, Lisbon, Comissão da Condição Feminina, 1991.

Relatório relativo à execução da convenção sobre a eliminação de todas as formas de discriminação contra a mulher,
— Comissão da Condição Feminina, Lisbon, 1982;
— Comissão da Condição Feminina, Lisbon, 1986;
— Comissão da Condição Feminina, Lisbon, 1988.

'Salário Mínimo', Ministério do Emprego e da Segurança Social — Departamento de Estatística, 1989, 1st semester 1991.

'A situação laboral da mulher em Portugal e na Espanha' (report by L. GARCIA ARIAS), *Perspectiva*, 4-8 July 1988, p. 8.

9.2 INFORMATION

9.2.1 ACTIVITIES OF THE COMISSÃO DA CONDIÇÃO FEMININA

May 1981
Literatura infantil: sua contribuição para um maior equilíbrio dos papéis em função do sexo, Lisbon.

March 1982
Igualdade no Trabalho (in collaboration with the Commission of the European Communities), Lisbon.

December 1983
Estudos sobre a mulher (with the support of the Calouste Gulbenkian Foundation), Lisbon.

November 1985
A Mulher e o Poder (in collaboration with the Department of Anthropology of the Universidade Nova de Lisboa and the support of the Embassy of France), Lisbon.

May 1986
Igualdade de oportunidades para as Mulheres (in collaboration with the Commission of the European Communities), Lisbon.

November 1986
Informação sobre o Fundo Social Europeu e Projectos para Mulheres (in collaboration with the Commission of the European Communities), Lisbon.

December 1986
A Mulher e o Ensino Superior, a Investigação Científica e as Novas Tecnologias em Portugal (in collaboration with the Junta Nacional de Investigação Científica Tecnológica), Lisbon.

January 1987
As Mulheres Agricultoras (in collaboration with the Commission of the European Communities), Caldas da Rainha.

July 1987
O Direito Comunitário e a Igualdade Jurídica entre Mulheres e Homens (in collaboration with the Commission of the European Communities), Lisbon and Porto.

November 1987
As Autarquias e a Informação às Mulheres (in collaboration with the Commission of the European Communities), Lisbon.

January 1988
A Igualdade de Oportunidades na Educação e Formação Profissional, Lisbon.

October 1988
Acções positivas em favor da igualdade (in collaboration with the Commission of the European Communities), Lisbon.

November 1988
Mulheres e Iniciativas de Emprego (in collaboration with the Institute of Employment and Professional Training (I.E.F.P.) and the Comissão para a Igualdade no Trabalho e no Emprego), Luso.

March1989
Informação às Mulheres nas Autarquias (in collaboration with the Commission of the European Communities), Coimbra and Porto.

April 1989
As Mulheres, a Identidade Cultural e a Defesa Nacional (in collaboration with the Instituto de Defesa Nacional), Lisbon.

May 1990
Igualdade, Democracia e Direitos Humanos (with the support of the Council of Europe, the Procuradoria-Geral da República, the Provedor de Justiça and the Instituto de Defesa Nacional), Lisbon.

November 1991
A Maternidade — Mitos e Realidades, Lisbon.

9.2.2 ACTIVITIES OF THE COMISSÃO DA CONDIÇÃO FEMININA AND ITS CONSULTATIVE COMMITTEE

June 1980
Década das Nações Unidas para a Mulher, Lisbon.

March 1984
A imagem da Mulher na Publicidade, Lisbon.

June 1985
Avaliação dos Resultados da Década das Nações Unidas para a Mulher em Portugal: estratégias para a futuro, Lisbon.

April 1987
As Mulheres e o Emprego em Portugal, Lisbon.

March 1988
A Revisão Constitucional e os Direitos das Mulheres, Lisbon.

May 1989
Assédio Sexual no Local de Trabalho, Lisbon.

June 1990
O emprego das mulheres e as estruturas de apoio à criança, Lisbon.

February 1991
Novas Tecnologias e Emprego das Mulheres, Lisbon.

May 1991
Participação Política e Democracia Paritária, Lisbon.

9.2.3 USEFUL ADDRESSES

Associação Portuguesa de Mulheres Juristas
Rua de S. Marçal, 77
1200 Lisboa

Comissão de Mulheres da União Geral de Trabalhadores (UGT)
Rua de Buenos Aires, 11
1200 Lisboa .... Tel. 397.65.05

Comissão Nacional das Mulheres da Confederação Geral dos Trabalhadores Portugueses - Intersindical Nacional (GTP-IN)
Rua Víctor Cordon, 1 - 3.°
1294 Lisboa Cedex .... Tel. 347.21.81

Comissão para a Igualdade no Trabalho e no Emprego
Av. da República, 44 - 2.°
1000 Lisboa .... Tel. 76.40.27

Comissão para a Igualdade e para os Direitos das Mulheres
Av. da República, 32 - 1.°
1093 Lisboa Cedex .... Tel. 797.60.81/4
.... Tel. 797.29.65 Library

Rua Ferreira Borges, 69 - 2.° C
4000 Porto .... Tel. 200.38.48 Library

INDEX

ACCESS
— to benefits, facilities, services 34
— to employment 31-32
— to promotion 34
— to training 33-34
ADVERTISEMENTS 31, 68
AGE OF RETIREMENT 20, 28, 44
AUTHENTICITY 29

BENEFITS
— post-employment 22
— unemployment 41
BREADWINNER 43
BURDEN OF PROOF 47-48

CASE LAW 81-98
— equal pay 81-88
— equal treatment 89-92
— equality in general 81
— equality in social security 93-98
CLASS ACTIONS 50
COLLECTIVE AGREEMENTS 54-55, 67
COLLECTIVE REDRESS 54-55
COMPARATOR 23, 31
COMPARISON
— cross-industry 23
COMPENSATION 49, 54
CONDITIONS OF WORK 32-33, 37
CONSTITUTIONAL LAW 3-4, 6-7, 9-10, 13, 38-39, 59-61
CONTEMPORANEOUS EMPLOYMENT 23
CONTRIBUTIONS
— by employee 22
— by employer 22
COSTS 48
COURTS AND TRIBUNALS 47-51
CRIMINAL SANCTIONS 49

DECENCY 29
DECLARATION 49
DETERMINING FACTOR, SEX AS A, ...28-30, 44-45
DETRIMENT 14-15
DIRECT DISCRIMINATION 14-16
DIRECT EFFECT
— of directives 7-8
— of EEC Treaty 7
DISCIPLINARY SANCTIONS 34
DISCRIMINATION
— by employee 35
by trade union 35
— definition of 13-14, 63
— direct 14-16
— indirect 16 18
— instruction to discriminate 35

DISCRIMINATION (continued)
— practices 35
— pressure to discriminate 35
DISMISSAL 34-35
DISPROPORTIONATE IMPACT 17
DOMESTIC EMPLOYEES 21, 30
DRESS CODES 16

EDUCATION AND TRAINING 33-34
EMPLOYEES
— discrimination by 35
— domestic 21, 30
— status of 20, 30
ENFORCEMENT 47-55
ENFORCEMENT AGENCY 52-54
EQUAL PAY 19-26
— case law 81-88
— exceptions 19-20
— legislation 66-67
— personal scope 20-21
— proportionate 25
EQUAL TREATMENT 27-39
— activities covered 31
— case law 89-92
— exceptions 27-30
— legislation 67-74
— personal scope 30-31
— territorial scope 30
EQUAL VALUE 24-25
ESTABLISHMENT
— different 23
EVIDENCE
— acquisition of 47
— prescribed forms 47
EXCEPTIONS
— to equality in social security 44-45
— to equality of pay 19-20
— to equality of treatment 27-30

FAMILY STATUS 15
FRINGE BENEFITS 22

GENUINE OCCUPATIONAL QUALIFICATION 29

HEALTH AND SAFETY 20, 27, 89-92
HEIGHT 25
'HIGHER VALUE' 25
HIRING 31-32
HOME WORKERS 21
HYPOTHETICAL MALE 23

INDEPENDENT CONTRACTORS 20, 30
INDIRECT DISCRIMINATION 16-18
INSTRUCTION TO DISCRIMINATE 35
INTERNATIONAL ORGANIZATIONS 6-7, 61-62

JOB
— classification ... 24-25
— description ... 32
— evaluation ... 24-25
— title ... 32
JUSTIFICATION OF DISCRIMINATION ... 18

LABOUR INSPECTORATE ... 52
LABOUR MARKET ... 4-5
LEGAL AID ... 48
LEGISLATION ... 10-12, 63-79
— equal pay ... 11-12, 66-67
— equal treatment ... 11-12, 67-74
— social security ... 12, 74-76
LEVELLING UP / DOWN ... 26, 45

MARKET FORCES ... 25
MARITAL STATUS ... 15, 17
MATERNITY ... 36
MILITARY SERVICE ... 27-28

NATIONAL SECURITY ... 20, 27-28
NIGHT-WORK ... 17, 24, 25, 76
NON-EMPLOYED PERSONS ... 21, 30
NULLITY ... 48

OBJECTIVE JUSTIFICATION ... 18
OCCUPATIONAL SOCIAL SECURITY ... 41

PARENTAL LEAVE ... 36
PART-TIME WORK ... 25-26, 45
PENSIONS ... 22
PORTUGUESE LEGAL SYSTEM ... 3-4
POSITIVE
— action ... 37-39
— action plan ... 49
— enforceable order ... 49
POST-EMPLOYMENT BENEFITS ... 22
PREGNANCY ... 15, 36
PRESSURE TO DISCRIMINATE ... 35
PRIVACY ... 29
PROMOTION ... 34
PROPORTIONATE PAY ... 25
PROTECTIVE LEGISLATION ... 36-37
PUBLIC SECTOR ... 21, 30

RECOMMENDATION ... 49
RECRUITMENT
— advertisements ... 31, 68
— methods ... 31-32
— selection ... 32
— terms ... 32
RELIGION ... 20, 28, 29
REMEDIES ... 48-49
REMUNERATION ... 21-22, 63
RETIREMENT AGE ... 20, 28, 44

SECURITY
— defence forces 27-28
— national 20, 27-28, 29
— social 41-45
SELECTION ARRANGEMENTS 32
SEXUAL HARASSMENT 15-16, 35
SOCIAL SECURITY 41-45
— case law 93-98
— exceptions 44-45
— legislation 74-76
— occupational 41
— statutory 41
SPECIAL TREATMENT 36-39
SPECIALIZATION 50-51
SPECIALIZED TRAINING 51

TIME LIMITS 50
TRAINING
— access to 33-34
— bodies 33-34

UNEMPLOYMENT BENEFITS 41

VALUE
— equal 24-25
— higher 25
VICTIMIZATION 18

WORK
— conditions of 32-33, 37
— hours of 17
— identical (equal pay) 23
— of equal value 24-25
— of higher value 25
— outside jurisdiction 19, 27
— part-time 25-26, 45
— relation to pay 32-33
— similar (equal pay) 23